Better Homes and Gardens®

Casual Entertaining

COOK BOOK

On the cover: At a backyard picnic, serve easy-to-fix foods and beverages. Feature *Sausage Sandwich, Bacon-Wrapped Fish Kebabs, Fruit Punch,* and *Strawberry Cooler.* Offer fresh fruit for dessert. (See index for recipe pages.)

BETTER HOMES AND GARDENS® BOOKS
Editor: Gerald M. Knox
Art Director: Ernest Shelton

Food and Nutrition Editor: Doris Eby
Senior Food Editor: Sharyl Heiken
Senior Associate Food Editors: Sandra Granseth, Elizabeth Woolever
Associate Food Editors: Bonnie Lasater, Marcia Stanley, Joy Taylor, Diana Tryon
Recipe Development Editor: Marion Viall
Test Kitchen Director: Sharon Golbert
Test Kitchen Home Economists: Jean Brekke, Kay Cargill, Marilyn Cornelius, Maryellyn Krantz, Marge Steenson

Associate Art Directors: Neoma Alt West, Randall Yontz
Copy and Production Editors: David Kirchner, Lamont Olson, David A. Walsh
Assistant Art Director: Harijs Priekulis
Senior Graphic Designer: Faith Berven
Graphic Designers: Alisann Dixon, Linda Ford, Tom Wegner

Editor in Chief: James A. Autry
Editorial Director: Neil Kuehnl
Group Administrative Editor: Duane Gregg
Executive Art Director: William J. Yates

Casual Entertaining Cook Book
Editor: Sandra Granseth
Copy and Production Editor: Lamont Olson
Graphic Designer: Sheryl Veenschoten
Consultant: Flora Szatkowski

CONTENTS

P·A·R·T·Y PLANNING THE BASICS

Everyone knows one host or hostess who can throw a great party with little apparent effort. The secret? Good planning eliminates those last-minute problems. With a practical menu and a congenial group of people, your party can be easy for you and fun for your guests.

You don't need a special occasion to plan a party. Just wanting to see friends is reason enough. But there are countless other reasons: birthdays, celebrations, holidays, new neighbors, and sporting events are all naturals. With a theme behind your get-together, friends, food, and fun are easier to plan.

Put together your guest list, then ask yourself a few questions:

Will my house comfortably accommodate this number of people? Can I serve this gathering? Can I afford to invite this many people? Is the type of party realistic?

If the answer to any of these is "no," you can find an alternate location, select a serving style that will help, cut down the guest list, or choose another theme.

If space is your problem, consider an outdoor party or one at a rented hall or room. Or serve guests in the living room, family room, kitchen, or basement in addition to the dining room. Borrow the extra tables and chairs, and set each table with a different colored tablecloth.

The size of the group will affect the serving style you choose. Buffets and cocktail parties lend themselves to a large number of guests. Sit-down dinners are more easily handled with smaller groups of people.

When the expense is your problem, serve lunch or brunch rather than a more expensive dinner, appetizers or dessert rather than a meal. Or, ask guests to bring part of the food or beverage.

With these thoughts in mind, decide on the type of party you'll have. Will it be a cocktail party, complete dinner, early brunch, afternoon tea, picnic in a park, or dessert and coffee in your living room? Location, time of day, date, and any entertainment you might include (sports, games, films, dancing) also determine the kind of party.

Once you have decided on the date, time, and occasion, invite your guests in writing or call them up on the telephone. A week ahead of the party is not too soon. Start earlier, 10 to 14 days before the party, if possible.

In the invitations, be sure to include a map or directions, an indication of the occasion, type of party, and what to wear, along with the time, date, and place.

Now you're ready to plan the party menu and work out a workable time schedule so you can pull off a successful party—and have a good time.

Menu Planning

Because you should spend your time with guests rather than alone in the kitchen, plan a menu that includes some items you can prepare well in advance. Round out your meal with simple, easy-to-fix foods. Of course, most menus do include a few dishes that require some last-minute attention, but with planning you can keep them to a minimum.

When choosing your menu, keep in mind the tastes and eating habits of your guests. A dieting guest is placed in an awkward situation when faced with a table full of calorie-laden foods. And try to be aware of the food allergies that your guests may have. If you don't know the preferences and health concerns of your guests, plan a menu that provides as much variety as possible, especially when you want to serve something unusual or uncommon.
Basic considerations in planning a menu center on appearance, taste, and practicality. Serve foods that contrast in texture, look, temperature, and taste.

On the other hand, too much contrast causes conflict. A spicy chili dip can spoil the taste of a delicate sauce. Two intense foods battle for attention, distracting from the merits of both.

Imagine how the food will be served on the plate. Are colors complementary? Are foods too bulky or too small for the plate? Will a garnish be needed to set off the foods?

It's always a good idea to plan your menu around foods you *know* you prepare well. If you want to serve a

new recipe, try it out on your family first for a preparation rehearsal and a chance to taste it. You might like to add your own personal touches once you know how it looks and tastes.

Let the occasion suggest menu ideas. Serve international foods at a bon voyage party, decorate a red, white, and blue cake on the Fourth of July, or serve shiny apples at back-to-school time.

As you plan, consider the time required to prepare each dish. Usually one or two complicated foods are plenty and they benefit from being accompanied by simpler dishes.

If you won't have much time, consider asking guests to bring part of the menu. Offer your recipes or ask them to make their own choices.

Another way to get help with food preparation is to make it part of the entertainment. Plan a participation party where you bring guests into the kitchen to chop, fry, toss, and flambé. It's fun to cook with a friend or two. For a few ideas, see the menu on page 8.

It's permissible to serve store-bought food at a party; it can make up the entire menu or serve as accompaniment for your homemade specialties. For appetizers, pick up egg rolls at a Chinese take-out or fancy hors d'oeuvres at a delicatessen. A deli is a great source for quantities of salads, luncheon meats, and cheese trays, too. For an easy meal ending,

buy a fancy dessert at a bakery or a distinctive flavor of ice cream at an ice cream shop. Keep in mind the specialties of the shops in your area, and use them to your advantage.

Once you have planned the entire menu, take inventory of serving utensils and accessories. Don't count on the same plate to serve both salad and dessert. Buy, rent, or borrow extra pieces well in advance of the event. Using your imagination, you'll find serving pieces you didn't know existed: a vase to hold breadsticks or vegetable dippers, an attractive coaster to hold a cheese ball or whipped butter.

Don't worry about matching china and flatware perfectly. An eclectic array of pieces could be a conversation starter. Remember paper plates and napkins for children's parties, outdoor affairs, and other casual events.

For more casual entertaining ideas, see the six menus on pages 8 through 13. They show how to use your time efficiently and give helpful suggestions to make entertaining easy for you and fun for your friends.

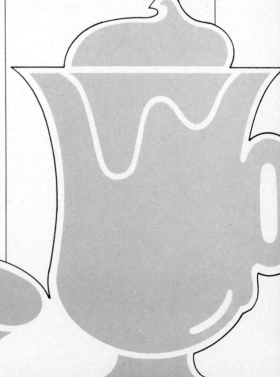

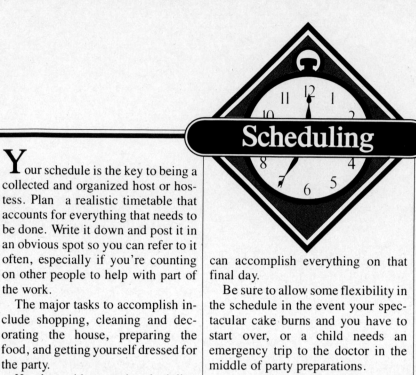

Scheduling

Your schedule is the key to being a collected and organized host or hostess. Plan a realistic timetable that accounts for everything that needs to be done. Write it down and post it in an obvious spot so you can refer to it often, especially if you're counting on other people to help with part of the work.

The major tasks to accomplish include shopping, cleaning and decorating the house, preparing the food, and getting yourself dressed for the party.

Here's a guide to use in scheduling your party preparations, but your own schedule may be very different, depending on the menu and the type of party. You may be able to prepare all the food in advance and eliminate all the last-minute chores. Even if you must be away from home until the day of the party, with help you can accomplish everything on that final day.

Be sure to allow some flexibility in the schedule in the event your spectacular cake burns and you have to start over, or a child needs an emergency trip to the doctor in the middle of party preparations.

Two or three days before: Do the bulk of shopping now, saving only highly perishable items for purchase later. Make a thorough list, referring often to the recipes you'll use and to the pantry shelves.

In addition to food, buy cleaning supplies, party favors, flowers or other decorations, liquor, and ice. Add paper plates, cups, and napkins if you plan to use them.

Get the house in order, doing the time-consuming jobs first, so all it takes is a quick "once-over" on the day of the party.

One day before: Prepare as much of the food as you can to avoid last-minute panic. Chop vegetables for use in cooking and refrigerate them in plastic wrap. Some foods, especially raw fruits and some vegetables for salads, are best cut up directly before serving. However, you can have them washed and ready in the refrigerator to chop or slice.

Check your recipes again to be sure you have all the ingredients and equipment you need. Make the final trip to the grocery store for last-minute items, if necessary.

Several hours before: Finish light housecleaning tasks. Arrange extra tables and chairs and set the table as far ahead of time as you like. Add centerpieces, candles, place cards, and favors. If the weather is cold or wet, make sure your closet or a bedroom will accommodate coats and umbrellas.

Begin the final cooking so all will be finished at the same time. Wash dishes as you go, so the cleanup won't take long. Set out serving dishes and utensils.

Clear a spot for placing used dishes as the diners finish with them, and provide for an easily accessible place for garbage. Make sure everything that needs chilling is in the refrigerator or a cooler.

One hour before: Put all the finishing touches on the meal and tables. Now take some time to relax a little, get dressed, and prepare to enjoy the party.

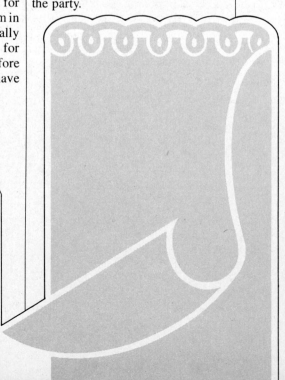

Making A Party Special

Parties offer an opportunity to show off your creativity and style in a variety of ways. Use your ingenuity to personalize your party. Here are a few ideas to get you started.

Garnishes: Perk up a platter of roast or hors d'oeuvres with a sprig of parsley or a wedge of citrus fruit. If strawberries or avocado slices complement your food and color scheme, add them to the plates.

Cut carrots, radishes, celery, and green onions into straight or ruffled sticks or fans to set off a relish tray.

For a pretty dessert garnish, balance a spiral of orange peel or a slice of kiwi fruit on the edge of a stemmed dessert or cocktail glass.

Even a sprinkle of paprika or a dollop of mayonnaise or whipped cream improves the appearance of some foods.

Centerpieces: Keep in mind that a centerpiece should accent a table, not interfere with guests. As long as you keep it away from eye level, almost anything goes.

Traditional fresh or dried flowers are always appropriate, but try some new arrangements in a basket or simply tied with a ribbon, lying flat on the table.

A bowl of fruit, a tray of fruit and cheese, or a dish of candy can make an edible centerpiece.

Or select other items that are special to you. Ceramic figures, candles, or bowls full of seashells or colored glass balls are possibilities.

Hot and cold: Serve hot foods on warmed plates to keep them warm longer. Heat the dinner plates in a 200° oven for a few minutes before taking them to the table.

Chill glasses for cocktails in the freezer or a bucket of ice. Place the salad dishes or sherbet glasses in refrigerator or freezer. Keep buffet foods cold by placing the bowl of cold food in a larger bowl of ice. Add mint leaves or flowers to the ice for a refreshing effect, or make the ice from colored water.

Doubling up: Make decorations and housecleaning count double by planning two parties for the same weekend or week; for instance a Saturday brunch followed by a Sunday open house. Be sure to plan for most of the food to be made ahead of time, and allow time to recover between parties. But you'll be surprised at the time and money you can save.

Drop-in guests: You can make unexpected guests feel welcome without hassle if you're always prepared. Keep the ingredients for a few quick-to-fix meals on hand (see menu, page 32). If you have no time to cook, don't apologize for serving take-out food. It's the company and atmosphere that are important.

Here's a way to entertain and cook at the same time. Wait till your guests arrive, and let them help with the preparation and the cooking! Most people enjoy cooking together, and even novices quickly learn to chop vegetables or mix up Tempura batter.

Schedule: Prepare the cake, salad dressing, and cheese spread a day ahead of time. Then organize your kitchen for the extra people who'll be using it. Be sure you have enough knives, cutting boards, and other utensils for all the cooks.

The tasks to be assigned are: cutting vegetables and meat for Tempura, slicing fruits for salad, and making the tempura batter and sauces. Set up 3 teams of 2 or 3 people and assign a team to work on each task. Don't assign yourself to a

---

HERBED CHEESE SPREAD*
ASSORTED CRACKERS

TEMPURA*

LEMON-POPPY SEED
FRUIT BOWL*

COCONUT CAKE RING*

HOT TEA   SAKE

---

team; you'll be needed to supervise, find things, and prepare beverages for the workers.

Provide each team with a copy of the recipe and the tools for the task. Arrange equipment in each team's working space. Move a team out of the kitchen for more space, if necessary. Be sure to provide garbage containers for the trimmings.

One hour before guests arrive,

wash vegetables and fruits; take out other ingredients. Set out cheese spread and assorted crackers to appease hungry appetites.

When all the food is cut and mixed, use 1 or 2 metal fondue pots or electric woks. Set them in the middle of the dining table. Each guest selects and cooks his own favorite vegetables and meats.

Alternative ideas: This type of participation party can work with many kinds of foods. Try a similar set-up with Beer-Cheese Fondue* or Crab-Cheese Fondue.*

Choose salad, appetizer, and dessert according to the main dish you select. To reduce preparations, buy one or more meal accompaniments (a frozen cake or ready-made dip). Serves 8.

*See index for page numbers.

After downhill sledding, skiing, or a movie on a cold winter's night, welcome your guests with an easy yet hearty meal. The advantage of this selection is that all the dishes can be made in advance and then the beef soup simply requires reheating.

Schedule: The day before or early on the day of the party, prepare the soup, bread, slaw, and flan. Have the table set and dishes ready before you leave home.

When you and guests arrive at the same time, all you have to do is reheat the soup and set out the rest of the meal. If you like, wrap bread in foil and reheat in a 400° oven about 15 minutes.

Alternate idea: Soups and stews often improve on reheating, so they are good choices for a gathering in which you arrive at the same time as

---

BEEF-NOODLE SOUP*

WHOLE WHEAT HONEY BREAD*

CHEESE OR BUTTER

FESTIVE COLESLAW*

CLASSIC CARAMEL FLAN*

WINE   COFFEE

---

your guests. Lamb Curry* and Beef Carbonnade* are good alternatives.

Substitute a fruit and gelatin salad for coleslaw, if you prefer; try Layered Pear Salad* or Sparkling Melon Ring.* For dessert, serve something simple to complement the rest of the meal. Apricot-Spice Bars* or a plate of fruit and cheese are possibilities.

When you can't cook ahead: There's another way to cook when you arrive with your guests—cook it fast and cook it simple.

For example, prepare Broiled Fish au Gratin* in a few minutes. Serve with sliced fresh tomatoes and purchased frozen yogurt or ice cream for dessert.

Veal Piccatta* cooks quickly, too. Round out the meal with a tossed salad, wild rice prepared from a mix, and Strawberries Romanoff* for dessert.

When it's hot outside, turn to Ham Roll-Ups* with no cooking at all. Assemble an assortment of fresh fruit and cheeses to double as salad and dessert. Add brown-and-serve rolls or bakery croissants with butter to complete the meal. Serves 6.

*See index for page numbers.

CURRIED CHICKEN SPREAD*

PUMPERNICKEL BREAD

ITALIAN CHEESE STICKS*

MIXED NUTS

APRICOT-SPICE BARS*

ALMOND THUMBPRINTS*

FRUITED CHAMPAGNE
PUNCH*

COFFEE

Y ou can easily serve 20 to 30 guests by yourself with this menu, because all the food can be prepared in advance and served buffet-style. If you plan on a small group, omit one or two foods. For a larger group, add more items.

Schedule: Start a day or two before the party and prepare all the food. Tightly cover the chicken spread and keep it in the refrigerator; chill the fruit juices for the punch and the champagne separately.

About one hour before the guests arrive, arrange the cheese sticks and cookies on serving plates. Set out the nuts and arrange sliced pumpernickel bread around the chicken spread. (If you prefer, use the spread to make sandwiches on white, whole wheat, or pumpernickel bread, then cut into quarters and arrange on a plate.) Set food on a buffet table in a location out of the main traffic pattern.

About 10 minutes before serving time, make coffee and prepare the punch in the punch bowl. Serve beverages from a separate table to avoid congestion, or right next to the food if your group is small. Then join guests for conversation.

Alternate ideas: Substitute sweets or snack foods that are easy to serve on a buffet for any of these menu items. You might include Fruit-Cheese Dip,* Mushroom Spread,* or Coffee-Chocolate Chip Bars.*

Serve Raspberry Punch* for a nonalcoholic alternative, if desired. When temperatures outside are cold, offer a warm punch, like Glögg.* Serves 25.

*See index for page numbers.

DINNER

When you invite someone special to dinner, splurge on a meal like this one. The foods here are familiar, but each has an unusual and sophisticated touch.

Schedule: The day before, make the Charlotte Russe and Raspberry Sauce. Prepare the pâté and chill. Mix sour cream and horseradish for sauce; refrigerate.

About 2½ hours before serving, begin cooking the roast; add potatoes to oven after 30 minutes. Assemble salad ingredients in a salad bowl and the dressing in a skillet.

Thirty minutes before serving time, remove potatoes; mash with remaining ingredients and restuff shells. Prepare vegetable dish. Whip

---

CHICKEN LIVER PÂTÉ*
ASSORTED CRACKERS

ROAST BEEF WITH
HORSERADISH SAUCE*

FRESH SPINACH SALAD*

WINE-BUTTERED
VEGETABLE MEDLEY*

BAKED POTATOES
ELEGANTE*

CHARLOTTE RUSSE*

WINE   COFFEE

---

the cream and fold into the horseradish-sour cream mixture.

Arrange crackers around pâté on a

serving platter. Serve with wine to guests in the living room, while you put finishing touches on the meal.

Heat salad dressing and pour over salad. Arrange vegetables and potatoes on serving plates.

At the table, carve the roast; pass horseradish sauce and vegetables family-style.

Alternate ideas: Another good choice for the meal would be Ham in Cottage Cheese Pastry.* Serve the ham with Maple-Sauced Yams.*

A colorful salad that can be made completely ahead is Vegetable Salad Medley.* For a spectacular finish to the meal, prepare Fruit Flambé* at the table. Serves 10.

*See index for page numbers.

Greet the first warm weather of spring with a barbecue that goes beyond franks and burgers. From the first sumptuous bite of seafood to the last creamy morsel of mousse, the food and outdoor air make an unbeatable combination.

Schedule: Begin by preparing the salad and dessert the day before. Mix marinade for seafood, then add seafood and refrigerate.

The day of the party, take all equipment outdoors and set up tables. Slice and butter a French bread loaf and wrap it in foil. Clean asparagus so it is ready to cook.

Before you go out to fire up the grill, read the manufacturer's instructions. Light the charcoal about 30 minutes before you plan to serve the appetizer. The coals are ready for grilling when black areas disappear

*GRILLED SHRIMP
AND SCALLOPS**

ORANGE-RUM HAM*

*CURRIED LAYERED
VEGETABLE SALAD**

ASPARAGUS SPEARS

BUTTERED FRENCH BREAD

FROZEN MOCHA MOUSSE*

ICED TEA   BEER

and coals look ash-gray by day and glow red after dark.

After guests arrive, grill shrimp, scallops, and mushrooms. Turn onto a plate and offer cocktail picks. While guests enjoy these, grill the ham, heat the sauce right on the grill. Place bread on edge of grill about 15 minutes before ham is done; turn of-

ten. Cook asparagus in boiling salted water for 10 to 15 minutes.

Serve ham and bread directly from the grill; pass salad and asparagus at the table.

Alternate ideas: Kebabs are good barbecue choices because they are easy to serve and taste terrific. Try Curry-Basted Pork Kebabs* or Herbed Lamb Kebabs* for a change of pace. Cold salads and desserts provide refreshing contrast to barbecued flavors. Marinated Cucumbers* and Frozen Pumpkin Pie* are welcome choices. Serve fresh corn-on-the-cob in place of asparagus.

If your barbecue is rained out: Just move everything indoors. Broil appetizer and ham steak in your oven approximately the same amount of time they·would grill. Serves 6.

*See index for page numbers.

Cocktails

The easiest kind of party to have when you want to invite a large group of people is a cocktail party. The variety of food makes preparation fun, and you need only enough room for your friends to stand.

Schedule: Prepare meatballs anytime before the party and freeze till needed. The day before the party, fix the nuts and shrimp dip. Survey bar supplies and make sure you have what you need (see page 88 for more information).

One hour before the party, cut up vegetables and arrange them on a tray. Arrange several types of cheese and crackers on another tray. Place serving pieces on buffet table. Shortly before guests arrive, prepare the chili dip and finish the meatballs. Place in fondue pots, chafing dishes, or on a warming tray.

GLAZED MEATBALLS*

CHILI CON QUESO*
TORTILLA CHIPS

DEVILED NUTS*

DILL-SHRIMP DIP*
VEGETABLE DIPPERS

CHEESE AND CRACKERS

MIXED DRINKS
SOFT DRINKS

Now spend some time mixing drinks, or appoint a friend or two to help you.

Alternate ideas: Any food goes at a cocktail party, as long as you can eat it without using a knife and fork. Variety is the key. Serve some hot and some cold foods, some hearty and some light. Suggestions are

Rumaki,* Italian Pizza Snacks,* and Green Goddess Dip.*

Cutting costs: When a tight budget figures prominently in party planning, don't panic. You have several alternatives. Cut your food cost by asking friends to bring food to the party. Offer your guests particular recipes or suggest that they bring their specialty.

Another way to save is to ask guests to provide their own liquor. You supply mixers, ice, and glasses, and guests bring their favorite liquors and brand names.

Or, instead of having an open bar, serve a liquor-based punch. Liquor is stretched, and you won't end up with an expensive bar bill. Vodka Punch* and Julep Punch* are good choices. Serves 16.

*See index for page numbers.

13

MAIN DISHES

Clockwise from left: Tempura,
Mustard Sauce, and Sweet-Sour Sauce
(see recipes, page 28)

Roast Beef with Horseradish Sauce *is featured in the menu on page 11.*

As a variation, serve the roast cold with the same sauce. Accompany the meat with a tossed green salad and Spicy Green Beans *(see recipe, page 46) for a quick and cool summer meal.*

ROAST BEEF WITH HORSERADISH SAUCE

1 4- to 6-pound boneless beef round rump roast	¼ teaspoon salt
¼ cup dairy sour cream	¼ teaspoon sugar
2 tablespoons grated fresh *or* prepared horseradish	Dash ground nutmeg
	½ cup whipping cream
	Snipped chives (optional)

Sprinkle meat with salt and pepper. Place, fat side up, on rack in roasting pan; insert meat thermometer. Roast in 325° oven for 2 to 2½ hours or till thermometer registers 150° to 170°. Let stand 15 minutes before carving. Meanwhile, combine sour cream, horseradish, salt, sugar, and nutmeg. Let mixture stand at room temperature while meat cooks. To serve, beat whipping cream to soft peaks; fold into horseradish mixture. Garnish with chives, if desired; pass with roast. Makes 10 to 12 servings.

SPICY MEAT PLATTER

1 4-pound beef chuck pot roast	½ cup dry red wine
2 tablespoons all-purpose flour	2 tablespoons red wine vinegar
2 tablespoons cooking oil	1 tablespoon brown sugar
3 small onions, cut into wedges	1 clove garlic, minced
½ cup raisins *or* currants	¼ teaspoon ground cinnamon
⅓ cup sliced pimiento-stuffed olives	¼ teaspoon ground cloves
1 6-ounce can tomato paste	¼ teaspoon ground cumin
	Hot cooked noodles

Coat meat with mixture of flour, 1 teaspoon *salt,* and dash *pepper.* In Dutch oven brown meat on all sides in hot oil. Add onions, raisins or currants, and olives. Combine remaining ingredients except noodles; pour over meat. Cover; roast in 325° oven 2½ to 3 hours or till tender, adding a little water, if needed. Remove meat to cutting board; slice thinly. Skim fat from pan juices. Arrange noodles on platter; top with meat and juices. Serves 8.

VEAL PICCATA

1 pound veal leg round *or* veal leg sirloin steak	¼ teaspoon dried basil, crushed
3 tablespoons butter	¼ teaspoon salt
1 cup sliced fresh mushrooms	Dash pepper
3 tablespoons lemon juice	2 tablespoons snipped parsley

With mallet, pound meat to ¼-inch thickness. Cut veal into 4 pieces. In 10-inch skillet cook *half* of the veal in hot butter over medium-high heat 1 minute on each side. Remove to a heated platter; keep warm. Add more butter to skillet, if necessary; cook the remaining veal. Remove to platter; keep warm. To butter remaining in skillet add mushrooms, lemon juice, basil, salt, and pepper. Cover; cook 5 minutes or till mushrooms are tender. Stir in parsley; spoon over veal. Serve at once. Serves 4.

SAUSAGE-STUFFED LAMB ROAST

1 6-pound leg of lamb, boned and butterflied	½ cup long grain rice
½ pound bulk pork sausage	½ cup dry white wine
1 medium onion, chopped	½ cup water
1 clove garlic, minced	¼ cup raisins
½ cup slivered almonds *or* pine nuts	1 teaspoon instant chicken bouillon granules
	¼ teaspoon ground nutmeg

Pound lamb on the inner meat surface to ¾-inch thickness. In skillet cook sausage, onion, and garlic till sausage is done. Drain off fat. Add nuts and rice to skillet; cook and stir 2 minutes. Stir in wine, water, raisins, bouillon, and nutmeg. Bring to boiling; reduce heat. Cover and cook 12 to 15 minutes or till water is absorbed. Spread sausage mixture over lamb. Roll up, jelly-roll style, starting from longest side. Tie with string. Place on rack in shallow roasting pan. Insert meat thermometer into thickest part of meat. Roast in 325° oven about 2 hours or till thermometer registers 170°. Makes 12 servings.

HAM IN COTTAGE CHEESE PASTRY

1 5-pound fully cooked canned ham	2 tablespoons finely chopped onion
1 10-ounce package frozen chopped spinach, thawed and drained	¼ teaspoon salt
	1½ cups all-purpose flour
½ cup grated Parmesan cheese	½ teaspoon salt
⅓ cup cooking oil	½ cup shortening
¼ cup very finely chopped almonds	¾ cup cream-style cottage cheese, sieved
	1 beaten egg

Place ham on rack in shallow baking pan. Insert meat thermometer. Bake in 325° oven for 1¼ to 1½ hours or till meat thermometer registers 140°. Remove ham from oven; use baster to remove drippings from pan. Remove rack. Cool ham 20 minutes. Trim any excess fat from outside of ham.

Meanwhile, prepare the filling. Place spinach between a double thickness of paper toweling; press out excess moisture from spinach. In small mixer bowl combine spinach, Parmesan cheese, cooking oil, almonds, onion, and the ¼ teaspoon salt. Beat well, scraping sides of bowl continuously till mixture is the consistency of soft butter. Set aside.

To make pastry, in medium mixing bowl stir together flour and the ½ teaspoon salt. Cut in shortening till pieces are the size of small peas. Add cottage cheese. Toss with fork till all is moistened. Form into a ball. On a lightly floured surface roll out pastry to 15x12-inch rectangle.

Spread spinach mixture atop the ham. Drape the pastry over the ham, covering top and sides with pastry. Mold pastry to the shape of the meat. Trim extra pastry at bottom; cut slits in top. Cut decorations from the pastry trimmings and arrange over the top.

Brush pastry with the beaten egg. Bake in 450° oven for 10 to 15 minutes or till pastry is browned. Transfer to serving platter. If desired, garnish with sprigs of watercress. Makes 12 to 15 servings.

If you don't have the time to bone a leg of lamb for your dinner party, then order it boned and butterflied from your butcher. Or, we have an even easier solution: Simply serve a bone-in lamb roast with the sausage stuffing served along side. Bake, covered, in a 1½-quart casserole in 375° oven for 20 to 25 minutes.

To roast a bone-in leg of lamb, sprinkle the roast with salt and pepper. Insert a meat thermometer into center of roast, making sure the bulb does not touch bone. Place, fat side up, on rack in shallow roasting pan. Roast in 325° oven 2½ to 3¾ hours or till meat thermometer registers 160° for medium doneness. Let stand 15 minutes before carving.

Curry-Basted Pork Kebabs, Indonesian Beef Skewers, and Herbed Lamb Kebabs

CURRY-BASTED PORK KEBABS

1½ pounds boneless pork	1 teaspoon dried oregano, crushed
4 large carrots	½ teaspoon salt
2 small zucchini	⅛ teaspoon pepper
8 small whole onions, peeled	1 clove garlic, minced
4 teaspoons curry powder	⅔ cup cooking oil
1 teaspoon paprika	

Cut pork, carrots, and zucchini into 1-inch pieces. In saucepan cook carrots, covered, in small amount boiling salted water 15 minutes. Add onions; cover and cook 10 minutes more. For sauce, in small saucepan combine curry, paprika, oregano, salt, pepper, and garlic; stir in oil. Heat through. Thread pork and vegetables on 6 to 8 skewers. Grill over *hot* coals 10 to 12 minutes, turning once; baste often with sauce. Serves 6 to 8.

INDONESIAN BEEF SKEWERS

2 pounds beef sirloin *or* boneless lamb, cut into 1-inch pieces	Few drops bottled hot pepper sauce
¼ cup peanut butter	¼ cup water
2 tablespoons lime juice	2 tablespoons soy sauce
1 tablespoon molasses	3 bananas, cut into 1-inch slices

Thread meat on 6 to 8 skewers. For sauce, in saucepan combine peanut butter, lime juice, molasses, and pepper sauce. Stir in water and soy. Bring just to boiling, stirring constantly. Keep warm. Baste meat with sauce. Grill over *hot* coals 10 to 15 minutes, turning once; baste often with sauce. Thread banana slices on skewers; add to grill 3 minutes before end of cooking time. Makes 6 to 8 servings.

HERBED LAMB KEBABS

½ cup cooking oil	1 teaspoon dried thyme, crushed
½ cup chopped onion	¼ teaspoon pepper
¼ cup snipped parsley	2 pounds boneless lamb, cut into 1-inch pieces
¼ cup lemon juice	Onion wedges
1 clove garlic, minced	Green pepper squares
1 teaspoon salt	Sweet red pepper squares
1 teaspoon dried marjoram, crushed	

For marinade, combine oil, onion, parsley, lemon juice, garlic, salt, marjoram, thyme, and pepper; stir in lamb. Cover and chill 6 to 8 hours; stir occasionally. Drain lamb, reserving marinade. Cook onion wedges in small amount of boiling water for 5 minutes; drain. Thread lamb, onion, and pepper squares onto 6 to 8 skewers. Grill over *hot* coals 10 to 12 minutes, turning once; baste often with marinade. Makes 6 to 8 servings.

Cleaning up after a party can be a letdown, but not if you follow this plan. Prepare and serve all the food in disposable containers. Cleaning up will be as easy as filling a trash can. Even the grill in this photo is disposable. You can buy one at a grocery or hardware store for a low price.

Thread kebabs on bamboo skewers, cook them on the throwaway grill, and serve on colorful paper plates with plastic forks and cups. How could a party be simpler?

Leave the peel on bananas for grilling so they will hold their shape when heated. Peel them before eating.

Tantalize your guests with the aroma of Orange-Rum Ham *cooking over the coals. Be sure to check on page 12 where we give an outstanding backyard menu that features this grilled entrée.*

Making your food attractive is as important as good flavor when you're cooking for company. Give this barbecued ham slice that party flair with orange twists. Slice an orange ⅛ inch thick. Cut into center of the slice and twist ends in opposite directions. Lay the twists on the ham slice to make an impressive garnish.

ORANGE-RUM HAM

¼ cup frozen orange juice concentrate, thawed
¼ cup rum
2 tablespoons brown sugar
2 tablespoons honey
¼ teaspoon ground ginger
¼ teaspoon ground cinnamon
1 1½- to 2-pound fully cooked ham center slice, cut 1 inch thick

For sauce, in saucepan combine orange juice concentrate, rum, sugar, honey, ginger, and cinnamon. Simmer, uncovered, about 5 minutes, stirring once or twice. Slash fat edge of ham slice to prevent curling. Grill ham over *medium* coals for 10 to 15 minutes; brush occasionally with sauce. Turn and grill 10 to 15 minutes more, basting occasionally. Heat remaining sauce on edge of grill. Cut ham into slices and pour sauce over. Makes 6 to 8 servings.

PLUM-SAUCED BARBECUED RIBS

8 to 10 pounds pork spareribs
½ cup chopped onion
2 tablespoons butter *or* margarine
1 17-ounce can purple plums
1 6-ounce can frozen lemonade concentrate, thawed
¼ cup chili sauce
¼ cup soy sauce
2 teaspoons prepared mustard
1 teaspoon ground ginger
1 teaspoon Worcestershire sauce

Cut ribs into 2- or 3-rib portions. In large Dutch oven bring salted water to boiling; reduce heat. Simmer ribs, covered, for 45 to 50 minutes or till tender; drain. For sauce, in large saucepan cook onion in butter or margarine till tender. Drain plums, reserving syrup; remove pits and discard. Place plums and syrup in blender container or food processor; cover and process till smooth. Add plum puree and remaining ingredients to onions. Simmer, uncovered, 10 to 15 minutes, stirring occasionally. Grill ribs over *slow* coals about 25 minutes, turning 3 or 4 times and brushing often with sauce till well coated. Pass remaining sauce. Makes 8 to 10 servings.

HAM ROLL-UPS

½ cup whipping cream
2 tablespoons mayonnaise *or* salad dressing
1 tablespoon prepared horseradish
1 8¼-ounce can crushed pineapple, drained
8 slices boiled ham
4 ounces liverwurst
⅓ cup chopped sweet pickle

Whip cream; fold in mayonnaise or salad dressing and horseradish. Fold ⅔ of the mixture into pineapple. Set remaining mayonnaise mixture aside. Spread pineapple mixture on *4* of the ham slices. Roll up. Spread remaining ham slices with liverwurst, then with the reserved mayonnaise mixture. Arrange chopped pickle down center. Roll up. Serve one pineapple-filled and one pickle-filled ham roll to each. Makes 4 servings.

ROUND STEAK AU POIVRE

1 tablespoon whole black peppercorns	¼ cup butter
1 pound beef top round steak, cut 1 inch thick	¼ cup chopped green onion
	⅔ cup dry red wine
	2 tablespoons brandy

Coarsely crack peppercorns with mortar and pestle or with spoon in metal mixing bowl. Cut steak into 4 serving pieces. Place steak pieces on waxed paper. Sprinkle *each* with ¼ to ½ teaspoon of the cracked peppercorns; rub over meat and press in with heel of hand. Turn and repeat on other side.

In 10-inch skillet melt *2 tablespoons* of the butter. Cook steaks over medium heat to desired doneness, turning once. Allow 11 to 12 minutes total cooking time for medium doneness. Season steaks on both sides with salt. Transfer to heated serving platter; keep warm.

In same skillet cook onion in remaining 2 tablespoons butter 1 minute or till tender. Add wine; boil rapidly over high heat about 5 mintues to reduce wine mixture to half, scraping up browned bits from pan. Stir in brandy; cook 1 minute more. Pour over steaks. Makes 4 servings.

Add a spectacular flourish to your culinary repertoire by flaming Round Steak au Poivre at tableside for your special friends. You'll be able to rival the best of restaurants with these easy-to-follow directions.

Simply cook the steaks as directed in the recipe, then make the sauce at the table in an electric skillet or a blazer pan or chafing dish. After reducing the wine mixture, pour brandy into a small saucepan and warm over a burner till brandy almost simmers. Use a saucepan with a protected handle or hold it with a potholder. Light a long match and hold over saucepan to ignite brandy. Extinguish match. Pour over the sauce mixture. Stir, allow flames to subside, then serve immediately.

ORANGE-BROILED PORK CHOPS

6 pork loin *or* rib chops, cut ¾ inch thick	¼ cup orange juice
½ cup bottled steak sauce	2 tablespoons brown sugar
1 teaspoon finely shredded orange peel	6 orange slices, cut ⅜ inch thick

Place chops on unheated rack in broiler pan. Broil 4 inches from heat 10 minutes; turn and broil 5 minutes. Meanwhile, to prepare sauce, combine steak sauce, orange peel, juice, and sugar. Baste chops. Broil 5 minutes longer; baste again. Top each chop with an orange slice; broil 1 to 2 minutes or till heated through. Heat and pass remaining sauce. Serves 6.

BEEF CARBONNADE

4 slices bacon	1 teaspoon instant beef bouillon granules
2 pounds beef stew meat, cut into 1-inch pieces	1 teaspoon dried thyme, crushed
1 12-ounce can beer	¼ teaspoon pepper
4 large onions, sliced	3 tablespoons cornstarch
1½ teaspoons salt	3 tablespoons water
1 bay leaf	

In skillet cook bacon till crisp; drain, reserving 2 tablespoons drippings in skillet. Crumble bacon; set aside. Brown *half* of the beef at a time in drippings. Return all meat to skillet along with beer, onions, salt, bay leaf, bouillon, thyme, and pepper. Cover and simmer 1 hour or till done. Skim off fat. Combine cornstarch and water; add to skillet. Cook and stir till bubbly; cook 1 to 2 minutes more. Top with bacon. Serve with boiled potatoes or hot cooked noodles, if desired. Serves 6 to 8.

Greek-Style Supper

Greek Beef Stew*

Tossed Salad

Buttered Carrots

Greek Lemon Cake*

Coffee

Enjoy this hearty menu on a chilly winter day. Guests will be intrigued by the aroma as they walk in the door, and you'll have plenty of time to spend with them.

The morning of the party, bake the cake. About 2 hours before guests arrive, start cooking the stew. Prepare the salad and refrigerate it separately from the dressing you choose. Clean and slice carrots, so all you'll need to do is cook them.

Now all that remains is a trip to the kitchen to add onions to the stew and start cooking the carrots, then one more to thicken the stew and serve the food. Serves 6.

See index for recipe pages.

GREEK BEEF STEW

3 tablespoons cooking oil	1 bay leaf
2 pounds beef stew meat, cut into 1-inch pieces	2 inches stick cinnamon
2 large cloves garlic, minced	1 pound small whole onions, peeled
3 cups water	3 tablespoons cornstarch
¼ cup dry red wine	3 tablespoons cold water
¼ cup tomato paste	½ cup walnut halves
2 tablespoons brown sugar	¼ pound feta cheese, coarsely crumbled, *or* muenster *or* Monterey Jack cheese, cubed
2 tablespoons red wine vinegar	
1½ teaspoons salt	

In Dutch oven heat cooking oil. Add half of the beef, turning to brown on all sides; remove and set aside. Repeat with the remaining beef and the garlic. Return all meat to pan. Add the 3 cups water, the wine, tomato paste, sugar, vinegar, salt, bay leaf, and cinnamon. Bring to boiling; reduce heat. Cover and simmer 1 to 1½ hours. Add onions; simmer 30 minutes longer. Remove bay leaf and stick cinnamon. Combine cornstarch and the 3 tablespoons cold water; add to stew. Return to boiling, stirring constantly; cook and stir 1 to 2 minutes more. To serve, sprinkle with walnuts and cheese. Makes 6 servings.

LAMB CURRY WITH FRUITED RICE

2 slices bacon	1 tablespoon curry powder
2 pounds boneless lamb *or* pork, cut into 1-inch pieces	½ teaspoon salt
1 large onion, chopped	½ teaspoon ground cinnamon
1 large apple, peeled and chopped	1 cup water
2 stalks celery, chopped	1 cup dairy sour cream
1 clove garlic, minced	2 tablespoons cornstarch
	2 tablespoons snipped parsley
	Fruited Rice

In a 12-inch skillet cook bacon till crisp; drain, reserving drippings in skillet. Crumble bacon; set aside. Add *half* of the meat to hot bacon drippings, turning to brown on all sides; remove and set aside. Repeat with the remaining meat; remove and set aside. Add onion, apple, celery, garlic, curry powder, salt, and cinnamon to skillet. Cook and stir till onion is tender but not brown. Return meat to skillet; add water. Cover and simmer for 1 hour or till meat is tender. Skim off fat. Combine sour cream and cornstarch; gradually add about ½ cup pan juices to sour cream. Return all to skillet. Cook and stir till thickened and bubbly; cook and stir 1 to 2 mintues more. Transfer to serving bowl. Sprinkle with crumbled bacon and parsley. Serve with Fruited Rice. Makes 6 servings.

Fruited Rice: In saucepan combine 3 cups cold *water* and 1 teaspoon *salt;* bring to boiling. Stir in 1¼ cups long grain *rice,* ¼ cup snipped dried *apricots,* and ¼ cup *raisins.* Cover and cook over low heat for 15 to 20 minutes or till the rice is tender.

SWEET-SOUR PORK

¾ cup all-purpose flour
½ cup water
1 tablespoon soy sauce
1 egg white
1 pound boneless pork, cut into
  ¾-inch pieces
  Cooking oil for deep-fat
  frying
2 carrots, cut into julienne
  strips
1 green pepper, cut into ¾-inch
  squares
1 small onion, cut into wedges

1 clove garlic, minced
2 tablespoons cooking oil
1 cup chicken broth
¼ cup vinegar
3 tablespoons sugar
2 tablespoons catsup
1 tablespoon soy sauce
2 tablespoons cornstarch
2 tablespoons dry sherry or
  sake
1 8-ounce can water chestnuts,
  drained and sliced
  Hot cooked rice

In bowl stir together the flour, water, and 1 tablespoon soy sauce till smooth. Beat egg white till stiff peaks form. Fold in beaten egg white. Dip pork pieces into flour mixture to coat. Fry, a few at a time, in deep hot fat (375°) about 5 minutes or till golden. Drain on paper toweling.

For sauce, in wok or skillet stir-fry carrots, pepper, onion, and garlic in 2 tablespoons cooking oil for 3 to 5 minutes or till crisp-tender. Stir in broth, vinegar, sugar, catsup, and 1 tablespoon soy sauce. Bring to boiling. Stir together cornstarch and sherry or sake; stir into vegetable mixture. Cook and stir till thickened and bubbly. Stir in water chestnuts and fried pork; heat through and serve at once. Serve with rice. Makes 4 to 6 servings.

Avoid the last minute preparation steps of Sweet-Sour Pork by making it ahead of time. To keep the pork crisp, refrigerate the fried pork separately from the vegetable-sauce mixture.

To serve, arrange pork pieces on baking sheet. Bake in 400° oven for 5 to 10 minutes or till crisp and hot. Heat the sauce over medium-low heat; add hot pork and serve immediately.

STIR-FRIED BEEF AND VEGETABLES

1 pound beef top round steak
¼ cup soy sauce
1 tablespoon cornstarch
¼ cup water
2 tablespoons sake or dry
  sherry
1 tablespoon molasses
2 tablespoons cooking oil

1 large onion, thinly sliced
2 medium carrots, cut into
  julienne strips
4 cups torn fresh spinach leaves
1 cup fresh bean sprouts
1 cup sliced fresh mushrooms
  Hot cooked rice

Partially freeze beef. Slice beef very thinly across the grain into bite-size strips. Stir soy sauce into cornstarch; stir in water, sake or sherry, and molasses.

Preheat a wok or large skillet over high heat. Add oil. Add onion and carrots; stir-fry over high heat for 3 minutes. Add spinach, bean sprouts, and mushrooms; stir-fry for 2 to 3 minutes longer or till vegetables are crisp-tender. Remove vegetables from pan; add more cooking oil, if necessary. Stir fry *half* of the meat about 2 minutes or till just browned. Remove from wok; add remaining meat and stir-fry. Return all meat to wok. Stir soy sauce mixture; stir into wok. Cook and stir till thickened and bubbly. Stir in vegetables. Cover; cook till just heated through. Serve with rice. Makes 4 to 6 servings.

Chili Supper

Green Goddess Dip*

Vegetable Dippers

Chorizo-Beer Chili*

Corn-Rye Biscuits*

Lemonut Bars*

When you serve a cold weather supper to a crowd, make it easy on yourself with a one-dish meal. Just add an easy appetizer, salad, bread, and dessert.

Prepare the cookies the day before and chill. If you like, you can make the chili ahead and reheat it just before the party.

Otherwise, start the chili about 2 hours before you plan to eat. Or, if you prefer a less hearty entreé, make Beef-Noodle Soup *(double the recipe). Cut up vegetables for the dip, and make the* Green Goddess Dip *(double this recipe, too).*

About 45 minutes before mealtime, prepare the biscuits. Make this recipe using a large bowl and 4 times the ingredients so each guest can enjoy two biscuits.

Serve the meal buffet style with large glasses of beer. Serves 14.

*See index for recipe pages.

Another party idea is to have a soup party picnic-style! Ask families to join you with pots of their favorite soups. You provide beverages, cheese, and crackers. The more people you invite, the greater the variety and enjoyment.

If you're short of bowls and spoons (or even if you're not), dust off the camping gear and serve dinner on the patio.

CHORIZO-BEER CHILI

1 pound chorizo *or* Italian sausage, cut into ½-inch pieces	2 4-ounce cans green chili peppers, rinsed, seeded, and chopped
3 pounds beef stew meat, cut into ½-inch pieces	1 6-ounce can tomato paste
4 medium onions, chopped	2 teaspoons salt
2 cloves garlic, minced	½ teaspoon bottled hot pepper sauce
1 28-ounce can tomatoes, cut up	2 16-ounce cans pinto beans, drained
1 12-ounce can beer	Shredded cheddar cheese

In 6-quart Dutch oven or kettle brown the sausage on all sides; remove to a large bowl. Cook the beef, onions, and garlic in sausage drippings over high heat, *half* at a time. Stir mixture often; cook till beef is browned. Return mixture to Dutch oven. Stir in *undrained* tomatoes, beer, chili peppers, tomato paste, salt, and bottled hot pepper sauce. Bring to boiling; reduce heat. Cover and simmer for 1½ hours or till meat is done. Skim off fat, if necessary. Add beans; heat through. Ladle into bowls; garnish each serving with shredded cheese. Makes 14 servings.

BEEF-NOODLE SOUP

2 slices bacon	1 teaspoon dried marjoram, crushed
1½ pounds beef stew meat *or* boneless pork, cut into ½-inch cubes	½ teaspoon salt
1 cup chopped onion	¼ to ½ teaspoon pepper
1 clove garlic, minced	3 ounces medium noodles
3 10½-ounce cans condensed beef broth	2 medium carrots, bias sliced
5 cups water	1 4-ounce can sliced mushrooms, drained
1 cup dry white wine	1 10-ounce package frozen peas
1 bay leaf	3 tablespoons cornstarch
	Snipped chives

In Dutch oven cook bacon till crisp; drain bacon, reserving drippings. Crumble bacon and set aside. Cook the beef or pork, onion, and garlic, *half* at a time, in drippings till meat is browned. Return all meat and onion to Dutch oven; drain off fat. Add condensed beef broth, 5 cups water, wine, bay leaf, marjoram, salt, and pepper. Cover and simmer for 1 hour.

Stir in *uncooked* noodles, carrots, and mushrooms. Bring mixture to boiling; cover and simmer 5 minutes. Add frozen peas; simmer 5 minutes more or till noodles and vegetables are tender. Remove bay leaf. Stir together cornstarch and 3 tablespoons *cold water;* add to simmering soup. Cook and stir till soup is slightly thickened and bubbly. Ladle into soup bowls; sprinkle each serving with crumbled bacon and snipped chives. Makes 6 servings.

Shrimp and Okra Gumbo (see recipe, page 29), Chorizo-Beer Chili, Chicken-Rice Soup (see recipe, page 35), and Beef-Noodle Soup

SAUSAGE AND BROCCOLI LASAGNE

When making Sausage and Broccoli Lasagne *ahead of time for your dinner party, follow these suggestions for storing and baking. Assemble casserole as directed in the recipe, reserving the second half of mozzarella cheese. Cover with foil and refrigerate.*

Bake the chilled casserole in 375° oven for 1 hour. Uncover; add remaining mozzarella cheese. Bake 15 minutes longer or till heated through. Let stand 10 minutes before serving.

There is no need to preheat the oven when baking the chilled lasagne as directed above.

1 **pound bulk Italian** *or* **pork sausage** *or* **ground beef**	½ **teaspoon garlic powder**
1 **cup chopped onion**	2 **10-ounce packages frozen**
1 **15-ounce can tomato sauce**	**chopped broccoli** *or*
1 **4-ounce can mushroom stems and pieces, drained**	**spinach**
1½ **teaspoons sugar**	10 **ounces lasagne noodles**
1 **teaspoon dried oregano, crushed**	2 **beaten eggs**
1 **teaspoon dried marjoram, crushed**	2 **cups ricotta** *or* **cream-style cottage cheese**
	½ **cup grated Parmesan cheese**
	8 **ounces sliced mozzarella cheese**

In skillet cook meat and onion till meat is browned. Drain off fat. Stir in tomato sauce, mushrooms, sugar, oregano, marjoram, garlic, and ½ teaspoon *salt*. Boil gently, uncovered, 10 minutes or till thickened; stir occasionally. Cook broccoli or spinach according to package directions; drain well. Cook lasagne noodles according to package directions. Rinse in cold water; drain. Combine beaten eggs, ricotta or cottage cheese, Parmesan cheese, and drained broccoli or spinach.

Arrange *half* of noodles in greased 13 x 9 x 2-inch baking dish. Spread with *half* of ricotta mixture, *half* of meat mixture, and *half* of mozzarella. Repeat layers of noodles, ricotta, and meat. Cover with foil; bake in 375° oven 30 minutes. Uncover; add remaining mozzarella. Bake 15 minutes more or till hot. Let stand 10 minutes before serving. Serves 10.

SPAGHETTI AND MEATBALLS

Vary this all-purpose spaghetti sauce by using different kinds of meat. Instead of meatballs substitute: 2 pounds bulk Italian sausage, cooked and drained; 1 pound salami or pepperoni, chopped; 3 cups chopped cooked beef or chicken; or three 7-ounce cans minced clams (substitute the clam liquid for part of the water in the recipe).

2 **cups chopped onion**	2 **teaspoons salt**
1 **cup chopped carrots**	1½ **teaspoons dried oregano, crushed**
2 **cloves garlic, minced**	
1 **tablespoon cooking oil**	1½ **teaspoons dried basil, crushed**
2 **28-ounce cans tomatoes, finely chopped**	¼ **teaspoon pepper**
1½ **cups water**	24 **ounces spaghetti** *or* **linguine**
1 **6-ounce can tomato paste**	**Italian Meatballs**
2 **tablespoons snipped parsley**	**Grated Parmesan cheese**

In Dutch oven cook onion, carrots, and garlic in oil, covered, till onion is tender. Stir in *undrained* tomatoes, water, tomato paste, parsley, salt, oregano, basil, and pepper. Simmer, uncovered, 45 minutes; stir occasionally. Cook spaghetti or linguine in large amount boiling salted water 10 to 12 minutes; drain. Add Italian Meatballs to tomato mixture; heat through. Serve over hot spaghetti. Pass Parmesan cheese. Makes 10 servings.

Italian Meatballs: In bowl beat 2 *eggs;* stir in 1 cup grated *Parmesan or romano cheese,* one 5⅓-ounce can *evaporated milk,* ½ cup finely chopped *onion,* ½ cup fine *dry bread crumbs,* 1 teaspoon *salt,* and ¼ teaspoon *pepper.* Add 2 pounds *ground beef;* mix well. Shape into 1-inch balls. Bake meatballs in shallow pans in 350° oven for 20 minutes or till done. Drain off fat.

ZUCCHINI-SAUSAGE PIE

1 pound bulk Italian sausage	1 cup shredded Swiss cheese
1½ cups shredded zucchini	½ teaspoon salt
4 beaten eggs	¼ teaspoon pepper
1 cup ricotta *or* cream-style cottage cheese	Pastry for Single-Crust Pie (see recipe, page 62)

In skillet brown sausage; drain off fat. Press liquid from zucchini between a double layer of paper toweling. In bowl combine eggs, sausage, zucchini, cheeses, salt, and pepper. Line 9-inch pie plate with pastry; fill with egg mixture. Bake in 375° oven 45 to 50 minutes or till knife inserted near center comes out clean. Let stand 10 minutes before serving. Serves 6.

Leave the peel on the zucchini when you shred it. The peel adds color to the pie and saves you a few minutes preparation time.

SAUSAGE SANDWICH pictured on the cover

1 14-inch loaf Italian bread	6 ounces sliced mozzarella cheese
¼ cup butter *or* margarine, softened	6 ounces sliced salami *or* pepperoni
1 tablespoon prepared mustard	2 tomatoes, sliced (optional)
1 tablespoon snipped parsley	3 pickled sweet peppers, seeded and quartered
1 clove garlic, minced	
¼ teaspoon crushed red pepper	

Cut bread into ½-inch slices, cutting to but not through bottom crust. Combine butter, mustard, parsley, garlic, and red pepper; spread on cut sides of alternate bread slices. Cut cheese and meat to fit bread slices. Add cheese, meat, tomatoes, and sweet peppers to buttered slits. Place on baking sheet. Bake in 350° oven for 15 minutes or till crisp and hot. (Or, wrap in foil; grill over *medium* coals for 20 minutes, turning often.) Cut bread apart into sandwiches. Makes 6 servings.

Microwave cooking directions: Assemble sandwiches as above, *except* cut loaf in half crosswise. Wrap each half in paper toweling; cook *each half* in countertop microwave oven on high power 4 minutes; turn once.

DILL-CHEESE MEATBALLS

Savory Meatballs	1¼ cups milk
2 11-ounce cans condensed cheddar cheese soup	1½ teaspoons dried dillweed
	Hot cooked noodles

Place Savory Meatballs in a 2½-quart casserole. Combine soup, milk, and dillweed; pour over meatballs. Bake in 375° oven for 25 to 30 minutes or till heated through. Serve with hot cooked noodles. Makes 12 servings.

Savory Meatballs: In a bowl combine 3 beaten *eggs,* 2 cups soft *bread crumbs,* 2 cups finely chopped *apple,* ¼ cup chopped *onion,* ¼ cup snipped *parsley,* and 1 teaspoon *seasoned salt.* Add 2 pounds *ground beef;* mix well. Shape into 48 meatballs. Arrange meatballs in large baking pan. Bake in 375° oven for 25 minutes or till done. Drain on paper toweling.

Dill-Cheese Meatballs are great for last-minute company meals. With meatballs in the freezer and canned soup in the pantry, a meal can be ready in 1 hour.

Freeze baked meatballs on a baking sheet; remove and place in plastic bag. Seal and freeze. To serve, place frozen meatballs in 2½-quart casserole. Add soup-milk-dill mixture. Bake in 375° oven for 50 to 55 minutes, stirring once or twice.

An electric wok or fondue pot makes cooking Tempura at the table easy entertainment. Let each guest cook his own favorite meats and vegetables.

Or, let guests do all the cooking at a participation party. For details, see the menu on page 12.

TEMPURA pictured on pages 14-15

½ pound fresh *or* frozen halibut *or* other fish steaks	½ pound chicken breast, skinned and boned
½ pound fresh *or* frozen scallops	1 egg
Tempura Sauce	¾ cup ice water
Sweet-Sour Sauce	1 cup all-purpose flour
Mustard Sauce	1 tablespoon cooking oil
½ pound broccoli	½ teaspoon sugar
¼ pound fresh green beans	½ teaspoon salt
1 sweet potato, peeled	Cooking oil for deep-fat frying
1 medium onion	
¼ pound whole fresh mushrooms	

Thaw fish and scallops, if frozen. Prepare the sauces; set aside. Cut broccoli into bite-size pieces. Cut green beans into 2-inch lengths. Cut sweet potato into ¼-inch slices. Cut onion into slices and separate into rings. Halve any large mushrooms or scallops. Cut fish and chicken into 1-inch pieces. In bowl beat egg with rotary beater. Beat in ice water, flour, 1 tablespoon oil, the sugar, and salt just till moistened. Add 1 or 2 *ice cubes* to bowl; use batter immediately.

Heat 1½ inches cooking oil to 400° in a wok, deep-fat fryer, electric skillet, or fondue pot.

Add 1 teaspoon *salt*. Spear fish, chicken, or vegetable piece with fondue fork; swirl in batter. Fry in hot fat 2 to 3 minutes. Pass sauces; serve with hot cooked rice, if desired. Makes 8 servings.

Tempura Sauce: In saucepan mix ½ cup *water*, ¼ cup *soy sauce*, 2 tablespoons *dry sherry*, ½ teaspoon instant *chicken bouillon granules*, and ½ teaspoon *sugar* to boiling. Keep warm.

Sweet-Sour Sauce: In saucepan combine ½ cup packed *brown sugar* and 1 tablespoon *cornstarch*. Stir in ⅓ cup *vinegar*, ⅓ cup *chicken broth*, 1 tablespoon *soy sauce*, ¼ teaspoon *garlic powder*, and ¼ teaspoon ground *ginger*. Cook and stir till thickened and bubbly. Keep warm.

Mustard Sauce: Combine ½ cup prepared *mustard* and 3 tablespoons *soy sauce*. Serve at room temperature.

BACON-WRAPPED FISH KEBABS pictured on the cover

1 pound frozen fish fillets	16 small whole onions
4 teaspoons lemon juice	16 pineapple chunks
8 slices bacon, halved	16 cherry tomatoes
2 green peppers	½ cup bottled barbecue sauce

Partially thaw fish; cut into 16 bite-size pieces. Sprinkle fish with lemon juice, salt, and pepper. Partially cook bacon; drain off fat. Roll *each* fish piece with a half-slice of bacon, placing bacon on outside; secure with wooden pick. Cut green peppers into 1½-inch chunks. Cook onions in boiling water, covered, 5 minutes, adding pepper chunks during last 2 minutes of cooking. Drain; peel onions. Thread rolled fish, onions, pepper chunks, and pineapple on 16 short skewers, ending with tomatoes. Grill over *medium-hot* coals about 15 minutes; turn and baste often with barbecue sauce. Makes 4 servings.

SHRIMP AND OKRA GUMBO

¼ cup cooking oil	1 tablespoon Worcestershire
¼ cup all-purpose flour	sauce
1 cup chopped onion	1 teaspoon cayenne
1 cup chopped celery	1 teaspoon dried thyme,
½ cup chopped green pepper	crushed
2 cloves garlic, minced	½ teaspoon salt
1 28-ounce can tomatoes,	½ teaspoon ground allspice
cut up	2 bay leaves
1 10-ounce package frozen cut	1 pound fresh *or* frozen shelled
okra, thawed	shrimp
¾ cup water	½ pint shucked oysters, cut up
1 tablespoon instant chicken	¼ cup snipped parsley
bouillon granules	Hot cooked rice

For roux, in large saucepan or Dutch oven mix oil and flour. Cook, stirring often, over medium-low heat for 15 minutes or till roux is dark brown. Stir in onion, celery, green pepper, and garlic; cook till vegetables are just tender. Stir in *undrained* tomatoes, okra, water, bouillon granules, Worcestershire, cayenne, thyme, salt, allspice, and bay leaves. Bring to boiling; reduce heat. Cover; simmer about 20 minutes. Remove bay leaves. Stir in shrimp, oysters, and parsley. Bring to boiling; reduce heat. Cover; simmer for 5 minutes. Serve over hot cooked rice in soup plates. Pass filé powder and bottled hot pepper sauce, if desired. Makes 6 servings.

Chicken and Okra Gumbo: Prepare Shrimp and Okra Gumbo as above, *except* substitute 2 cups cubed cooked *chicken* for the shrimp.

Serve gumbo in the best of Cajun style. Heat shallow soup plates in a 200° oven or rinse with hot water and dry quickly. Then, mound cooked rice in the center of each plate. Spoon gumbo around the rice and serve. Pass filé powder and hot pepper sauce for those who like the more authentic Louisiana flavor.

When preparing this gumbo be sure to stir the roux constantly during the browning process. Once it begins to brown the color turns quickly and the mixture may burn.

SALMON QUICHE

1 cup whole wheat flour	1 cup dairy sour cream
⅔ cup shredded cheddar cheese	¼ cup mayonnaise *or* salad
¼ cup finely chopped almonds	dressing
½ teaspoon salt	½ cup shredded sharp cheddar
¼ teaspoon paprika	cheese
6 tablespoons cooking oil	1 tablespoon grated onion
1 15½-ounce can salmon	¼ teaspoon dried dillweed
3 beaten eggs	3 drops bottled hot pepper
	sauce

For crust, stir together flour, the ⅔ cup cheese, almonds, salt, and paprika. Stir in oil. Set aside ½ *cup* of the crust mixture. Press remaining mixture into bottom and sides of 9-inch pie plate. Bake in 400° oven 10 minutes. Remove from oven; reduce oven temperature to 325°.

For filling, drain salmon, reserving liquid. Add water to reserved liquid, if necessary, to make ½ cup liquid. Flake salmon, removing bones and skin. Mix eggs, sour cream, mayonnaise, and reserved salmon liquid. Stir in salmon, the ½ cup cheese, onion, dillweed, and pepper sauce. Spoon into crust. Sprinkle with reserved crust mixture. Bake in 325° oven for 45 minutes or till firm in center. Makes 6 servings.

Broiled Fish au Gratin

BROILED FISH AU GRATIN

6 fresh *or* frozen fish fillets (1½ pounds)	¾ cup soft bread crumbs
¼ cup butter, melted	¼ cup grated Parmesan cheese
	2 tablespoons snipped parsley

Thaw fish, if frozen. Arrange on greased rack of unheated broiler pan. Brush with *2 tablespoons* of the butter. Broil 4 inches from heat 5 to 10 minutes or till fish flakes easily when tested with fork (allow 5 to 6 minutes for each ½ inch of thickness). Mix crumbs, cheese, and parsley. Add remaining 2 tablespoons butter; toss well. Sprinkle over fish. Broil 1 to 2 minutes more or till browned. Pass lcmon wedges, if desired. Makes 6 servings.

Sometimes simple foods are the most welcome. Serve Broiled Fish au Gratin *on a bed of sautéed shredded zucchini with a garnish of halved cherry tomatoes and lemon wedges.*

Accent this colorful plate with festive place mats and napkins tied in decorative knots.

FISH ROLL-UPS HOLLANDAISE

6 fresh *or* frozen fish fillets	½ teaspoon dried tarragon, crushed
2 tablespoons chopped shallots *or* green onion	¼ teaspoon salt
2 tablespoons butter	⅛ teaspoon pepper
1 10-ounce package frozen chopped spinach, thawed and drained	¼ cup dry white wine *or* water
	2 lemon slices
	Easy Hollandaise Sauce

Thaw fish, if frozen. In skillet cook shallots or green onion in butter till tender. Remove from heat; stir in spinach, tarragon, salt, and pepper. Lay fish fillets on flat surface; spread spinach evenly onto fish. Roll up jelly roll fashion, starting with short end. Secure with wooden picks, if necessary. Arrange rolls seam side down in 10-inch skillet. Add wine or water and lemon. Cover and simmer 12 to 15 minutes or till fish flakes easily when tested with fork. Transfer to platter; top with Easy Hollandaise Sauce. Makes 6 servings.

Easy Hollandaise Sauce: In blender or food processor mix 2 *egg yolks,* 1 tablespoon *lemon juice,* and ⅛ teaspoon *salt.* Cover and blend till combined. Heat 6 tablespoons *butter* till bubbly. Turn on machine; immediately pour hot butter slowly into running blender or food processor. Blend till all butter is added and sauce is thick. Serve immediately.

FISH STEAKS WITH MUSHROOMS

6 to 8 fresh *or* frozen halibut *or* other fish steaks	1 small green pepper, chopped
3 cups thinly sliced fresh mushrooms	½ cup dry white wine
2 green onions, thinly sliced	¼ cup lemon juice
1 medium tomato, chopped	1 teaspoon salt
	½ teaspoon dried dillweed
	⅛ teaspoon pepper

Thaw fish, if frozen. Arrange in greased 13x9x2-inch baking dish. Top with mushrooms, onions, tomato, and green pepper. Combine wine, lemon juice, salt, dillweed, and pepper; pour over fish. Cover; bake in 350° oven 25 minutes or till fish flakes easily when tested with fork. Remove fish with spatula; top with vegetable mixture. Makes 6 to 8 servings.

Fish Steaks with Mushrooms *fill your need for an entrée to serve dieting guests. With no added fat and lots of tasty vegetables, it's a dish calorie counters (and big eaters) can appreciate. Serve with green beans, a fresh fruit salad, and breadsticks to make a light yet satisfying meal.*

Keep the ingredients for this simple meal on hand for all the times visitors drop in unexpectedly. It's simple but satisfying, and can be put together in about an hour.

Prepare the muffins about 1 hour before serving time; while they bake, assemble the fish casserole. Remove the muffins from oven; reduce oven temperature to 375° and add the casserole.

Toss the salad a few minutes before serving; reheat the muffins in the oven the last few minutes of casserole cooking time.

Don't worry about the fondue till you're through eating the main course; it goes together quickly with the help of a frozen pound cake. Serve leftover fondue on ice cream. Serves 4 to 6.

*See index for page numbers.

CURRIED FISH CASSEROLE

1 **16-ounce package frozen fish fillets**	1 **teaspoon curry powder**
	Dash pepper
¼ **cup chopped onion**	1 **cup shredded cheddar,**
2 **tablespoons butter**	**American,** *or* **Swiss cheese**
1 **10¾-ounce can condensed cream of mushroom** *or* **cream of celery soup**	1 **16-ounce can French-style green beans, drained**
	¾ **cup soft bread crumbs**
½ **cup milk**	1 **tablespoon butter, melted**

Cook fish according to package directions; drain. Break into chunks. Cook onion in 2 tablespoons butter till tender. Add soup, milk, curry, pepper, and ½ *cup* of the cheese; stir till cheese melts. Combine fish and beans in 10x6x2-inch baking dish. Pour soup mixture over. Mix remaining cheese, crumbs, and 1 tablespoon melted butter; sprinkle atop. Bake in 375° oven for 20 to 25 minutes. Makes 4 to 6 servings.

SOLE PROVENÇALE

6 **fresh** *or* **frozen sole** *or* **flounder fillets**	1 **3-ounce can chopped mushrooms, drained**
¼ **cup butter** *or* **margarine**	¼ **cup dry white wine**
1 **16-ounce can tomatoes, cut up**	¼ **cup chopped onion**
	1 **clove garlic, minced**

Thaw fish, if frozen. Dot *each* fillet with *2 teaspoons* of the butter; sprinkle with salt and pepper. Roll up fillets; fasten with wooden picks, if necessary. Place rolls in 10-inch skillet. Add *undrained* tomatoes, mushrooms, wine, onion, and garlic. Cover and simmer 15 minutes or till fish flakes easily when tested with a fork. Remove fish to warm platter; keep hot. Cook tomato mixture, uncovered, over high heat 10 minutes or till thickened. Spoon over fish. Garnish with lemon wedges, if desired. Makes 6 servings.

CURRY ROAST CHICKEN

½ **cup chopped onion**	⅓ **cup raisins**
½ **cup chopped celery**	¼ **teaspoon pepper**
1 **teaspoon curry powder**	1 **cup chicken broth**
¼ **cup butter** *or* **margarine**	1 **4- to 5-pound whole roasting chicken**
5 **cups dry bread cubes**	
⅓ **cup chopped cashews**	**Cooking oil**

Cook onion, celery, and curry in butter or margarine till tender. Stir in bread cubes, cashews, raisins, pepper, and ½ teaspoon *salt*. Add broth; toss to mix. Rub neck and body cavities of chicken with salt; spoon bread mixture loosely into cavities. Skewer neck skin to back. Tie legs to tail. Twist wing tips under back. Place chicken, breast side up, on rack in shallow roasting pan. Brush with oil. Roast in 375° oven for 2 to 2½ hours; baste occasionally with pan juices. Makes 4 servings.

FRUIT-STUFFED CORNISH HENS

4 to 6 1- to 1½-pound Cornish game hens
⅓ cup chopped onion
⅓ cup chopped celery
1 tablespoon butter *or* margarine
1 16-ounce can whole cranberry sauce
1 12-ounce can fried rice

1 8-ounce can crushed pineapple, drained
¼ teaspoon ground ginger
1 8-ounce can unpeeled apricot halves, drained
½ of an 8-ounce can water chestnuts, drained
Soy sauce

Sprinkle hen cavities with salt. Cook onion and celery in butter till tender. Stir in cranberry sauce, rice, pineapple, and ginger. Chop apricots and water chestnuts; stir in. Spoon mixture loosely into cavities. Tie legs together. Place in shallow roasting pan; cover with foil. Bake in 375° oven 30 minutes. Uncover; bake 1 hour more. Baste with soy the last 30 minutes. Serves 4 to 6.

Bake the stuffing that won't fit into the Cornish hens in a small casserole to serve as a side dish. Cover the casserole and bake with the hens for the last 45 minutes.

ORANGE-WINE SAUCED TURKEY BREAST

1 5- to 6-pound frozen breast of turkey, thawed
⅔ cup orange juice
⅓ cup dry white wine
2 tablespoons cooking oil
1 tablespoon snipped chives

1 clove garlic, minced
1 teaspoon instant chicken bouillon granules
¼ teaspoon ground allspice
⅛ teaspoon pepper
¼ cup all-purpose flour

Place turkey on rack in shallow roasting pan; insert meat thermometer. Roast in 325° oven for 2½ to 3 hours or till thermometer registers 185°. Mix orange juice, wine, oil, chives, garlic, bouillon, allspice, and pepper. Baste turkey occasionally with orange mixture. Remove turkey to platter; let stand 15 minutes. Pour pan juices into 4-cup measure; skim off fat. Add remaining wine mixture and enough water to make 2¼ cups; stir into flour. Cook and stir till bubbly; cook 1 to 2 minutes more. Season; pass with turkey. Serves 10.

ALMOND-CHICKEN CASSEROLE

1 9-ounce package frozen French-style green beans
1 8-ounce package wide noodles
1 8-ounce carton plain yogurt
½ cup mayonnaise
¼ cup dry white wine
½ teaspoon salt

½ teaspoon dried parsley flakes
½ teaspoon dried dillweed
¼ teaspoon garlic powder
3 cups cubed cooked chicken
1 cup slivered almonds
⅓ cup grated Parmesan cheese

Cook beans and noodles separately, according to package directions; drain well. In bowl combine yogurt, mayonnaise, wine, salt, parsley, dill, garlic powder, and dash *pepper*. In 3-quart casserole layer *half* of the noodles, beans, chicken, almonds, cheese, and yogurt mixture; repeat. Bake, covered, in 350° oven 45 minutes. Makes 6 to 8 servings.

Make cooking for 20 relatives as easy as possible. Prepare this whole menu before the family arrives, or prepare just the entrée yourself and ask other family members to bring the rest.

The day before, pound chicken breasts and prepare stuffing mixture; chill separately. Mix the cereal coating. Make the salad.

The day of the party, prepare the beans and cook in crockery cooker about 4 hours ahead of time. Then, 1¼ hours before serving, assemble chicken dish and bake.

A few minutes before mealtime all you have to do is put garnishes on the food and serve. Serves 20.

*See index for page numbers.

FRUITED CHICKEN ROLLS

1 cup fine dry bread crumbs	3 cups whole bran cereal, crushed
1 cup finely snipped dried apricots	⅔ cup shelled sunflower seed, chopped
1 cup finely chopped walnuts	½ cup butter, melted
1 cup light raisins	3 tablespoons lemon juice
2 tablespoons finely chopped onion	½ teaspoon salt
1 teaspoon ground allspice	10 whole large chicken breasts, halved lengthwise and boned
1 teaspoon dried thyme, crushed	
¾ to 1 cup chicken broth	

For stuffing, in large bowl combine bread crumbs, snipped apricots, walnuts, raisins, onion, allspice, and ½ *teaspoon* of the thyme; mix well. Add enough broth to moisten stuffing as desired. Set aside.

In small bowl combine cereal, sunflower seed, and remaining ½ *teaspoon* thyme. Combine melted butter, lemon juice, and salt. Place chicken breasts, skin side down, on board between 2 pieces of plastic wrap. With meat mallet pound chicken from center to edge till ¼ inch thick. Cover and chill. About 1¼ hours before serving, place chicken pieces, skin side down; sprinkle with salt. Place about ¼ *cup* of the apricot stuffing on each breast; fold in sides of chicken and roll up from short end. Secure with wooden picks to form compact bundles. Brush each roll generously with melted butter mixture; roll in cereal mixture to coat. Place, seam side down, in two 13x9x2-inch baking pans. Bake in 375° oven for 40 to 50 minutes or till brown and crisp. Garnish with dried apricot halves and lettuce leaves, if desired. Makes 20 servings.

CHICKEN BREASTS SUPREME

2 tablespoons finely chopped green onion	⅛ teaspoon salt
2 tablespoons butter *or* margarine	⅛ teaspoon pepper
	1 tablespoon all-purpose flour
2 whole medium chicken breasts, skinned, halved lengthwise, and boned	¼ teaspoon dried rosemary, crushed
	¾ cup light cream
4 ounces fresh mushrooms, sliced *or* one 2½-ounce jar sliced mushrooms, drained	1 beaten egg yolk
	¼ cup dry white wine
	Paprika
	Snipped parsley

In skillet cook onion in butter or margarine for 2 minutes. Add chicken breasts and mushrooms. Cook over medium heat about 10 minutes or till chicken is done and lightly browned, turning once. Remove to warm platter; sprinkle with salt and pepper. Cover and keep warm. Stir flour and rosemary into skillet drippings; add light cream. Cook and stir till thickened and bubbly. Gradually add *half* of the hot mixture to egg yolk. Return mixture to pan; cook and stir over medium heat till thickened. Stir in wine. Pour over chicken. Sprinkle with paprika and parsley. Makes 4 servings.

CHICKEN JAMBALAYA

3	whole small chicken breasts, skinned, halved lengthwise, and boned	1	16-ounce can tomatoes, cut up
2	tablespoons cooking oil	1	cup dry white wine
1	large onion, chopped	2	tablespoons snipped parsley
1	large green pepper, chopped	1	bay leaf
2	cloves garlic, minced	½	teaspoon salt
⅔	cup long grain rice	½	teaspoon dried thyme, crushed
1	cup diced fully cooked ham	¼	teaspoon cayenne

In large skillet brown chicken breasts on both sides in hot oil; remove from skillet. Add onion, green pepper, and garlic to pan drippings; cook till tender but not brown. Stir in uncooked rice; cook and stir till rice is golden. Arrange chicken breasts atop rice mixture; sprinkle ham over all. Combine *undrained* tomatoes, wine, parsley, bay leaf, salt, thyme, and cayenne; pour over chicken. Do not stir. Bring to boiling; reduce heat. Cover and simmer for 20 minutes. Uncover and cook 5 minutes more or till chicken is tender and rice is done. Remove bay leaf before serving. Makes 6 servings.

Shrimp Jambalaya: Prepare recipe as directed above, *except* omit the chicken. Cook onion, green pepper, and garlic in oil; proceed as directed. Cook the rice-tomato mixture for 10 minutes, then stir in 1 pound fresh *or* frozen *shelled shrimp*. Cook, covered, 10 minutes more. Uncover and cook 5 minutes longer.

Traditional jambalaya is a magnificent Creole dish made from leftovers. But, for this spicy version, you don't need leftovers. Add a green salad and French bread for a satisfying meal.

Finish your dinner with Fruit Flambé,* a spectacular dessert that is popular in Louisiana restaurants where you'll find the best Creole cooking.

CHICKEN-RICE SOUP

1	3-pound broiler-fryer chicken, cut up	2	carrots, chopped (1 cup)
7	cups chicken broth	1	small turnip, chopped (½ cup)
2	stalks celery with tops, cut up	1	cup fresh *or* frozen cut green beans
1	medium onion, quartered	⅔	cup long grain rice
2	bay leaves	2	3-ounce packages cream cheese, cubed
½	teaspoon salt		
¼	teaspoon pepper		

In kettle *or* Dutch oven combine the chicken pieces, chicken broth, celery, onion, bay leaves, salt, and pepper. Bring mixture to boiling; reduce heat. Cover and simmer for 1 hour or till chicken is tender. Remove chicken from broth; set aside.

Strain broth, discarding celery, onion, and bay leaves. Skim off excess fat. Return broth to kettle; add chopped carrots, turnip, green beans, and uncooked rice. Cover and simmer 20 minutes or till rice is tender.

Meanwhile, remove skin and bones from chicken; discard. Cut chicken into chunks. Add to soup along with the cream cheese; cook and stir till cheese melts. Ladle into soup bowls. Makes 8 servings.

Hearty Brunch

Crusty Ham Soufflé*

Ambrosia*

*Cranberry Ladder
Coffee Cake**

Spiced Chocolate Sipper*

Having a brunch is a fun way to entertain. You can have a party and then have the whole afternoon and evening to relax and enjoy a favorite activity.

For this menu, bake the coffee cake the day before the party.

Start preparing the Ambrosia and soufflé about 1½ hours before the party. Put soufflé in the oven and you have 55 minutes before you need to pay attention to it. Prepare the beverage about 15 minutes before serving. Serves 6.

*See index for page numbers.

CRUSTY HAM SOUFFLÉ

2 tablespoons butter	3 tablespoons all-purpose flour
¾ cup finely shredded cheddar cheese	1 cup milk
¼ cup fine dry bread crumbs	4 eggs, separated
¼ cup wheat germ	1 3-ounce can sliced mushrooms
3 tablespoons butter	1 cup diced, fully cooked ham

Melt 2 tablespoons butter; stir in ¼ *cup* cheese, crumbs, and wheat germ. Press onto sides and bottom of 1½-quart soufflé dish. Melt remaining butter; stir in flour. Stir in milk. Cook and stir till bubbly. Stir in remaining ½ cup cheese. Remove from heat. Beat egg yolks till thick and lemon-colored. Slowly stir in milk mixture. Drain mushrooms; fold with ham into yolk mixture. Beat egg whites till stiff peaks form. Fold in ham mixture. Turn into prepared soufflé dish. Bake in 325° oven for 55 minutes. Serves 6.

MEXICAN CHEESE ENCHILADAS

1 7½-ounce can tomatoes	1 pound cheddar *or* Monterey Jack cheese, cut into 12 strips
2 4-ounce cans green chili peppers, rinsed and seeded	
1 clove garlic, cut up	¼ cup chopped green onions
¼ teaspoon ground coriander	1 large avocado, seeded
12 6-inch corn tortillas	½ cup dairy sour cream

In blender container place *undrained* tomatoes, *half* of the chilies, garlic, and coriander. Cover; blend till smooth. Chop remaining chilies; set aside. Pour tomato mixture into 8-inch skillet; bring to boiling. Remove from heat. Dip a tortilla into sauce; place a cheese strip on tortilla. Sprinkle with onion and chopped chilies. Roll up; place in 13x9x2-inch baking dish. Repeat with remaining tortillas. Pour remaining sauce over tortillas. Cover and bake in 350° oven 15 to 20 minutes. Peel and mash avocado; stir in sour cream and ¼ teaspoon *salt*. Pass with enchiladas. Makes 6 servings.

BRUNCH EGG TACOS

5 brown-and-serve sausage links, thinly sliced	¼ cup rinsed, seeded, and chopped canned green chili peppers
1 tablespoon finely chopped onion	6 taco shells
4 beaten eggs	Bottled taco sauce
¼ cup light cream *or* milk	½ cup shredded cheddar cheese

Brown sausage according to package directions; drain, reserving drippings. Cook onion in drippings till tender. Combine eggs, cream or milk, ½ teaspoon *salt,* and dash *pepper;* pour into hot skillet. Add sausage and chilies. Cook, stirring gently, till set but glossy. Spoon egg mixture into taco shells. Pour taco sauce over *each;* top with some of the cheese. Heat in 8x8x2-inch baking pan in 350° oven for 10 minutes. Serves 6.

SUMMER VEGETABLE OMELET

1½ cups thinly sliced zucchini or
    yellow summer squash
2 tablespoons sliced green
    onion
¼ cup butter or margarine
1 medium tomato, peeled,
    chopped, and drained

6 eggs
¼ cup milk
1 tablespoon snipped parsley
½ teaspoon salt
½ teaspoon dried oregano,
    crushed
¼ cup grated Parmesan cheese

In 10-inch oven-going skillet cook squash and onion in butter or margarine, covered, 5 minutes or till just tender. Add tomato; spread mixture evenly over skillet. Beat together eggs, milk, parsley, salt, and oregano; pour over vegetables. Cook, uncovered, over medium heat. As eggs set, run spatula around edge of skillet, lifting eggs so uncooked part can run underneath. When omelet is almost set, sprinkle with cheese. Bake in 400° oven 4 to 5 minutes or till top is set. Cut into wedges. Serves 6.

If you like, substitute chopped fresh broccoli for all or part of the zucchini in this recipe. Serve the omelet for breakfast, brunch, or a light supper.

AVOCADO AND EGG SANDWICHES

6 hard-cooked eggs, chopped
2 avocados, seeded, peeled, and
    chopped
1 cup mayonnaise
2 tablespoons curry powder

4 pita bread rounds, halved
    crosswise
2 tomatoes, chopped
4 cups shredded lettuce
½ cup alfalfa sprouts

In bowl combine eggs, avocados, mayonnaise, and curry powder. Spoon about ½ *cup* of the mixture into *each* of the pita halves. Top with tomato, lettuce, and alfalfa sprouts. Sprinkle with salt. Makes 4 servings.

Bacon and Egg Sandwiches: Prepare Avocado and Egg Sandwiches as above, *except* substitute 12 ounces *bacon,* crisp-cooked, drained, and crumbled, for the chopped avocado.

BEER-CHEESE FONDUE

1 clove garlic, halved
2 tablespoons butter
3 tablespoons all-purpose flour
1 tablespoon prepared mustard
1 12-ounce can beer
1 tablespoon Worcestershire
    sauce

1 pound sharp cheddar cheese,
    cubed
½ loaf rye bread, cut into 1-inch
    cubes
1 head cauliflower,
    crisp-cooked and broken
    into flowerets
1 pint cherry tomatoes

Cut cooked chicken or turkey into ½-inch cubes for additional dippers for Beer-Cheese Fondue. *Add more color with cooked broccoli flowerets in addition to the cauliflower and tomatoes.*

Keep cooked vegetables warm and have tomatoes at room temperature for better flavor.

In saucepan cook garlic in butter over medium heat till garlic begins to brown. Discard garlic. Stir flour and mustard into butter. Add beer. Cook and stir till bubbly; cook and stir 1 to 2 minutes more. Stir in Worcestershire; gradually stir in cheese till melted. Transfer to fondue pot; place over fondue burner. Spear bread and vegetables on fondue forks; swirl in fondue to coat. Serves 6.

SIDE DISHES

Clockwise from top left: Lemon-Poppy Seed Fruit Bowl (see recipe, page 41). Whole Wheat Honey Bread (see recipe, page 53), Onion Buns (see recipe, page 49), Tossed Salad with Avocado Dressing (see recipe, page 40), Sparkling Melon Ring (see recipe, page 43), and Fresh Spinach Salad (see recipe, page 40)

A good selection of greens makes a salad really special. Choose from romaine, escarole, mustard greens, spinach, watercress, curly endive, and the many types of lettuce: bibb, iceberg, Boston, leaf, and red-tipped leaf.

TOSSED SALAD WITH AVOCADO DRESSING pictured on pages 38–39

1 small red onion	1 tablespoon lemon juice
1 small cucumber	2 teaspoons anchovy paste
6 cups torn salad greens	¼ teaspoon salt
1 avocado, seeded and peeled	⅛ teaspoon pepper
⅓ cup plain yogurt	2 tablespoons salad oil

Thinly slice onion and separate into rings; thinly slice cucumber. Toss onion and cucumber with greens in salad bowl. Cut up avocado; add to blender container or food processor with yogurt, lemon juice, anchovy paste, salt, and pepper. Cover and blend till nearly smooth. With machine running, gradually add oil. Blend smooth. If desired, add more oil to make a thinner consistency. Pour over greens; toss to serve. Makes 6 to 8 servings.

To prepare this salad ahead of time, assemble the vegetables and eggs in the salad bowl and keep in the refrigerator. Just before serving, cook the bacon and add to salad. Add dressing ingredients to the drippings in the skillet. At serving time, bring the dressing to boiling and pour over the salad. Serve immediately.

FRESH SPINACH SALAD pictured on pages 38–39

1 pound fresh spinach leaves, torn (12 cups)	6 slices bacon
3 cups sliced fresh mushrooms	⅓ cup cooking oil
1 8-ounce can water chestnuts, drained and sliced	¼ cup sugar
4 hard-cooked eggs, chilled and cut into wedges	¼ cup catsup
	¼ cup vinegar
	2 teaspoons Worcestershire sauce

Arrange spinach, mushrooms, water chestnuts, and eggs in a large salad bowl. In skillet cook bacon till crisp; drain, reserving drippings in pan. Crumble bacon over spinach. To drippings, add cooking oil, sugar, catsup, vinegar, and Worcestershire sauce. Bring to boiling; pour over salad and toss to mix. Makes 8 to 10 servings.

HERBED CARROT-POTATO SALAD

4 carrots, thinly bias-sliced	2 tablespoons snipped chives
8 medium potatoes, cooked, peeled, and sliced	1 tablespoon Worcestershire sauce
1 cup thinly sliced celery	1 teaspoon salt
½ cup sliced pitted ripe olives	½ teaspoon dried dillweed
1 cup mayonnaise *or* salad dressing	½ teaspoon dry mustard
1 cup dairy sour cream	⅛ teaspoon pepper
3 tablespoons lemon juice	Leaf lettuce

Cook carrots in small amount boiling water 2 minutes; rinse in cold water. Drain. In large bowl toss together carrots, potatoes, celery, and olives. Combine mayonnaise or salad dressing, sour cream, lemon juice, chives, Worcestershire, salt, dillweed, mustard, and pepper; mix well. Pour over vegetables; toss to coat well. Cover and chill several hours. Pile into lettuce-lined bowl. Garnish with carrot curls, if desired. Makes 12 servings.

CURRIED LAYERED VEGETABLE SALAD

6 cups torn lettuce	½ cup mayonnaise *or* salad
1 pint cherry tomatoes, halved	dressing
1 10-ounce package frozen	1 tablespoon snipped parsley
peas, thawed	1 tablespoon milk
1 medium cucumber *or*	1 teaspoon curry powder
zucchini, thinly sliced	½ teaspoon sugar
½ cup dairy sour cream	6 slices bacon, crisp-cooked
	and crumbled

In large bowl layer in order *3 cups* of the lettuce, the tomatoes, peas, remaining 3 cups lettuce, and cucumber or zucchini. Combine sour cream, mayonnaise, parsley, milk, curry, and sugar; spread atop cucumber, sealing to edge of bowl. Cover and chill up to 48 hours. Wrap and chill crumbled bacon. Just before serving, sprinkle with bacon. Serves 10.

Garnish this make-ahead salad to suit your taste. Instead of bacon, sprinkle it with sliced green onion, shredded cheddar cheese, grated Parmesan cheese, or finely chopped green pepper.

To show off the layers to your guests, prepare the salad in a straight-sided glass bowl.

FESTIVE COLESLAW

1 small head green cabbage,	½ cup chopped peanuts
coarsely shredded	½ cup mayonnaise *or* salad
1 small head red cabbage,	dressing
coarsely shredded	½ cup dairy sour cream
3 carrots, shredded	1 tablespoon honey
1 cup seedless green grapes,	1 teaspoon celery seed
halved	½ teaspoon salt

In large bowl combine cabbage, carrots, grapes, and peanuts. Stir together mayonnaise or salad dressing, sour cream, honey, celery seed, and salt. Pour over cabbage mixture; toss to mix. Cover and chill till serving time. Makes 16 to 18 servings.

LEMON-POPPY SEED FRUIT BOWL   pictured on pages 38–39

2 tablespoons honey	2 oranges
¼ teaspoon finely shredded	1 pint fresh strawberries
lemon peel	2 apples
2 tablespoons lemon juice	2 pears
1½ teaspoons poppy seed	2 bananas
¼ teaspoon dry mustard	2 peaches
Dash salt	2 cups seedless green grapes
⅓ cup salad oil	

For dressing, in small mixer bowl beat together honey, lemon peel, lemon juice, poppy seed, mustard, and salt. Gradually add oil, beating with electric mixer or rotary beater till mixture is thickened. Cover and chill. Chill fruit, except bananas. Peel and section oranges. Hull and halve strawberries. Slice apples and pears; peel and slice bananas and peaches. In large bowl combine all fruit; pour dressing over. Toss to coat. Makes 12 servings.

In the middle of the hot summer host a salad luncheon in the coolest spot in your house. Cover the buffet table with crisp linen dish towels, and serve the food in assorted kitchen ware. Use everything from mixing bowls to canisters, baking sheets, colanders, and measuring cups. (See photo, page 38.)

VEGETABLE-STUFFED AVOCADOS

½ **cup chopped cucumber**
½ **cup chopped fresh broccoli**
½ **cup sliced cauliflower**
2 **tablespoons chopped onion**

½ **cup Cucumber Dressing**
2 **avocados, halved and seeded**
Lemon juice

Combine cucumber, broccoli, cauliflower, and onion. Toss with Cucumber Dressing to coat. Cover and chill. Brush cut evocado surfaces with lemon juice. Trim a thin slice from bottom of each half. Fill with vegetable mixture. Serve on lettuce-lined plates, if desired. Makes 4 servings.

Cucumber Dressing: Stir together ½ cup *mayonnaise or salad dressing*, ½ cup dairy *sour cream*, and 2 tablespoons *milk*. Stir in ½ cup drained shredded *cucumber*, 1 tablespoon snipped *parsley*, 1 teaspoon *sugar*, 1 teaspoon *lemon juice*, ½ teaspoon *salt*, and dash *pepper*; mix well. Chill in covered container. Stir in additional *milk*, if needed. Makes 1½ cups.

VEGETABLE SALAD MEDLEY

1 **small head cauliflower, sliced (3½ cups)**
3 **cups thinly sliced carrots**
1 **10-ounce package frozen peas**
1 **8-ounce can water chestnuts, drained and sliced**
¼ **cup chopped green pepper**
2 **tablespoons chopped green onion**

½ **cup salad oil**
½ **cup vinegar**
1 **tablespoon sugar**
½ **teaspoon salt**
¼ **teaspoon dried basil, crushed**
¼ **teaspoon dried dillweed**
⅛ **teaspoon pepper**
1 **cup shredded cheddar cheese**

Cook cauliflower and carrots, covered, in boiling salted water 4 minutes; add peas. Cover and cook 2 minutes more. Drain and cool. Mix cooked vegetables, water chestnuts, green pepper, and onion. In screw-top jar combine oil, vinegar, sugar, salt, basil, dillweed, and pepper. Cover; shake well. Pour over vegetables and toss. Cover and chill. Just before serving, stir in cheese. Makes 10 to 12 servings.

MARINATED VEGETABLE SALAD

1 **cup sugar**
1 **cup Italian-style cooking sauce**
1 **cup vinegar**
½ **cup salad oil**
¼ **cup water**
2 **teaspoons salt**

½ **teaspoon pepper**
6 **carrots, sliced (3 cups)**
2 **medium cucumbers, sliced**
1 **small green pepper, cut into rings and halved**
1 **medium onion, sliced and separated into rings**

For marinade, in large bowl combine sugar, cooking sauce, vinegar, oil, water, salt, and pepper. Stir in carrots, cucumbers, green pepper, and onion to coat. Cover; chill several hours or overnight, stirring occasionally. Drain vegetables; serve in lettuce-lined bowl, if desired. Makes 8 servings.

LAYERED PEAR SALAD

1 **16-ounce can pear halves**	1 **teaspoon vinegar**
Cold water	1 **3-ounce package cream**
1 **3-ounce package**	**cheese, softened**
lemon-flavored gelatin	⅛ **teaspoon ground ginger**
1 **cup boiling water**	6 **to 12 walnut** *or* **pecan halves**

Drain pears, reserving syrup; add enough cold water to syrup to make 1 cup liquid. Chop pears; set aside. Dissolve gelatin in boiling water; stir in reserved pear liquid. Measure ⅔ *cup* of the gelatin mixture; set remainder aside. To the ⅔ cup gelatin, add vinegar; pour into a 4-cup mold. Chill till almost firm.

Meanwhile, beat cream cheese and ginger till fluffy; stir in remaining gelatin mixture. Chill mixture till partially set (consistency of unbeaten egg whites). Fold pears into cream cheese mixture. Arrange nuts upside-down on gelatin in mold; spoon pear mixture atop. Chill till firm; unmold. Serves 6.

SPARKLING MELON RING   pictured on pages 38–39

2 **envelopes unflavored gelatin**	2 **cups small honeydew melon**
1¼ **cups cold water**	*or* **cantaloupe balls**
1 **6-ounce can frozen lemonade**	2 **tablespoons sliced**
concentrate, thawed	**maraschino cherries**
2 **cups ginger ale**	¼ **cup dairy sour cream**
2 **tablespoons maraschino**	¼ **cup mayonnaise** *or* **salad**
cherry juice	**dressing**

In saucepan soften gelatin in ½ *cup* of the cold water; stir over low heat till gelatin dissolves. Remove from heat. Stir in remaining ¾ cup cold water and lemonade concentrate. Slowly add ginger ale. Divide mixture in half. Stir cherry juice into one of the halves; chill till partially set (consistency of unbeaten egg whites). Keep remainder at room temperature. Fold melon and cherries into partially set gelatin. Pour into a 6½-cup ring mold. Chill till almost firm.

Combine sour cream and mayonnaise; add to second half of gelatin mixture. Beat with rotary beater till smooth. Slowly pour over chilled gelatin. Chill overnight. Unmold onto platter. Fill center with curly endive and garnish with melon balls and cherries, if desired. Serves 8 to 10.

BLUE CHEESE AND APPLE SALAD

1 **3-ounce package**	½ **cup dairy sour cream**
lemon-flavored gelatin	1 **cup finely chopped apple**
1¼ **cups boiling water**	¼ **cup crumbled blue cheese**
¼ **cup dry white wine**	**(1 ounce)**

Dissolve gelatin in boiling water; stir in wine. Gradually blend into sour cream. Chill till partially set (consistency of unbeaten egg whites); fold in apple and cheese. Turn into 3-cup mold. Chill till firm. Unmold; garnish with celery leaves, if desired. Makes 4 to 6 servings.

GELATIN SALADS are easy to make when you know the basics. Just make sure your gelatin mixture is at the right consistency before proceeding to the next step.

Partially set gelatin is chilled to the consistency of unbeaten egg whites. Chill to this stage before you add fruit, nuts, or cheese so they will stay suspended in the gelatin mixture.

Almost firm describes gelatin that appears to be set, but remains sticky to the touch. To make layered salads, slowly pour or spoon the second layer over the first almost firm one.

Firm gelatin is completely set and no longer sticky to the touch. It can be unmolded onto the serving plate without falling apart.

To unmold a salad, loosen edges with a spatula. Dip mold in warm water up to the rim for a few seconds. Tilt the mold to ease gelatin away from the sides all the way around.

Invert the serving plate atop mold; turn plate and mold over together and shake gently till the salad falls onto the serving plate. Lift off the mold.

Garnish the salad with greens, celery leaves, or some fresh ingredients found in the salad. Prepare a little extra for the garnish.

There's no need to worry about preparing Creamed Mushrooms in Tomatoes *at the last minute. Assemble them ahead of time and chill till needed. Then bake the chilled tomatoes in a 350° oven for 20 to 25 minutes or till mushrooms are hot.*

Experiment with seasonings in the mushrooms, if you like. Substitute dried tarragon, crushed, or dried basil, crushed, for dillweed. They'll take on a different flavor, but one just as intriguing.

CREAMED MUSHROOMS IN TOMATOES

6 medium tomatoes
6 cups sliced fresh mushrooms
2 tablespoons sliced green onion
2 tablespoons butter
1 tablespoon all-purpose flour
1 tablespoon snipped parsley
½ teaspoon salt
½ teaspoon dried dillweed
Dash ground red pepper
½ cup light cream
⅓ cup rich round cracker crumbs (10 crackers)
2 teaspoons butter, melted

Cut thin slice from top of each tomato; scoop out seeds and pulp, leaving outside shell. Reserve pulp for another use. Sprinkle insides of tomatoes with a little salt; invert on paper toweling to drain. Cook mushroom and onion in 2 tablespoons butter 10 minutes or till most of liquid evaporates. Stir in flour, parsley, salt, dillweed, and red pepper. Cook; stir 1 minute more. Stir in cream; cook and stir till thickened and bubbly. Cook 1 minute more. Set tomatoes upright in 9x9x2-inch baking pan. Spoon mushrooms into tomatoes. Combine crumbs and 2 teaspoons melted butter; spoon over tomatoes. Bake in 400° oven 10 minutes or till crumbs are golden. Serves 6.

BROCCOLI WITH BLUE CHEESE

1 10-ounce package frozen cut broccoli
1 tablespoon butter
1 tablespoon all-purpose flour
Dash salt
½ cup milk
⅓ cup crumbled blue cheese
2 teaspoons prepared mustard

Cook broccoli according to package directions; drain well. Melt butter; stir in flour and salt. Add milk all at once. Cook and stir till bubbly. Continue 1 to 2 minutes more. Stir in cheese and mustard. Stir in broccoli; heat through. Makes 4 servings.

SPINACH-NOODLE CASSEROLE

10 ounces noodles
2 10-ounce packages frozen chopped spinach
2 1¾-ounce envelopes hollandaise sauce mix
1 teaspoon dry mustard
1½ cups water
2 cups dairy sour cream
½ cup grated Parmesan cheese
1 teaspoon salt
¼ cup Italian-seasoned bread crumbs
2 tablespoons grated Parmesan cheese
1 tablespoon butter *or* margarine, melted

Cook noodles and spinach separately according to package directions; drain. Combine sauce mix and mustard; stir in water. Cook and stir till bubbly; remove from heat and stir in sour cream. Set aside ¼ *cup* spinach. Stir remaining spinach, noodles, ½ cup Parmesan, and salt into sauce mixture. Turn into 12x7½x2-inch baking dish. Spread reserved spinach in center. Cover; bake in 350° oven 30 minutes. Combine crumbs, 2 tablespoons Parmesan, and butter; sprinkle in a ring around spinach. Bake, uncovered, 10 minutes more. Serves 8.

Creamed Mushrooms in Tomatoes
Spinach-Noodle Casserole

When you can't buy fresh spinach, substitute two 10-ounce packages frozen chopped spinach for the fresh spinach in this recipe. Allow it to thaw, then drain thoroughly before adding to the mushrooms.

MUSHROOM-SPINACH SAUTÉ

2 **pounds fresh spinach**
2 **cups sliced fresh mushrooms**
2 **tablespoons butter**
⅓ **cup whipping cream**

2 **tablespoons dry white wine**
½ **teaspoon salt**
¼ **teaspoon ground nutmeg**
Dash pepper

Wash, drain, and chop spinach. In saucepan cook mushrooms in butter till tender. Stir spinach into mushrooms. Cover and cook 5 minutes or till spinach is wilted. Stir in cream, wine, salt, nutmeg, and pepper. Heat through; serve at once. Makes 6 servings.

WINE-BUTTERED VEGETABLE MEDLEY

1 **10-ounce package frozen Italian green beans**
1 **10-ounce package frozen cauliflower**
2 **tablespoons butter**

2 **tablespoons dry white wine**
1 **tablespoon snipped parsley**
Dash pepper
2 **tablespoons broken pecans *or* walnuts**

Cook vegetables together according to package directions. Drain well. Add butter, wine, parsley, and pepper to vegetables in saucepan. Heat through, stirring gently. Turn into serving bowl; sprinkle with nuts. Serves 6.

Pass lemon wedges to squeeze over these Indian-style beans. Lemon gives them authentic flavor and extra taste appeal.

SPICY GREEN BEANS

2 **tablespoons cooking oil**
1 **teaspoon mustard seed**
2 **10-ounce packages frozen cut green beans**
1 **small onion, chopped**

1 **teaspoon ground coriander**
½ **teaspoon sugar**
½ **teaspoon salt**
Dash cayenne

In saucepan heat oil and mustard seed till seed pops. Stir in beans and onion; cover. Cook over medium heat 12 to 15 minutes or till beans are crisp-tender; stir often. Stir in remaining ingredients. Serves 6 to 8.

HERB-SCALLOPED CORN

1 **beaten egg**
1 **16-ounce can whole kernel corn, drained**
1 **8-ounce can cream-style corn**
1 **cup milk**

1 **cup shredded Swiss cheese**
½ **cup herb-seasoned stuffing mix**
1 **tablespoon chopped pimiento**
Dash pepper

Combine egg, drained corn, cream-style corn, milk, ¾ *cup* of the cheese, stuffing mix, pimiento, and pepper. Turn into 1½-quart casserole. Bake in 350° oven 40 minutes. Top with remaining cheese. Bake 5 to 10 minutes more or till set. Let stand 5 minutes before serving. Serves 4 to 6.

SPICY BACON-BEAN POT

3 16-ounce cans baked beans in tomato sauce	1 cup chopped red *or* green pepper
2 15-ounce cans red kidney beans, drained	¼ cup bottled smoke-flavored barbecue sauce
2 12-ounce cans whole kernel corn, drained	2 teaspoons chili powder
10 slices bacon, crisp-cooked, drained, and crumbled	¼ teaspoon garlic powder
1 cup chopped onion	½ cup shredded sharp cheddar cheese (2 ounces)

In Dutch oven combine beans, corn, bacon, onion, pepper, barbecue sauce, chili powder, and garlic powder. Cover and cook over medium heat 35 minutes, stirring occasionally. Sprinkle with cheese. Makes 20 servings.

Crockery cooker directions: In 3½-quart slow crockery cooker combine beans, corn, bacon, onion, pepper, barbecue sauce, chili powder, and garlic powder. Cover and cook on high-heat setting for 3½ to 4 hours, stirring once or twice. Sprinkle with cheese.

MAPLE-GLAZED YAMS

2 18-ounce cans sweet potatoes, drained	½ cup maple-flavored syrup
1 11-ounce can mandarin orange sections, drained	¼ cup slivered almonds, toasted
¼ cup raisins	3 tablespoons butter *or* margarine

Arrange sweet potatoes, oranges, and raisins in a 11x7x1½-inch baking pan. Pour maple syrup over sweet potato mixture; sprinkle with toasted almonds. Dot with butter or margarine. Bake in 325° oven for 30 to 40 minutes or till mixture is heated through. Makes 6 to 8 servings.

Microwave cooking directions: Assemble casserole as directed above. Cover with waxed paper. Cook in countertop microwave oven on high power for 8 to 10 minutes, turning once.

BAKED POTATOES ELEGANTE

5 medium baking potatoes	2 tablespoons butter *or* margarine, softened
½ cup dairy sour cream	1 teaspoon onion salt
1 3-ounce package cream cheese, softened	⅛ teaspoon white pepper
2 tablespoons milk	2 tablespoons diced pimiento

Bake potatoes in 325° oven for 90 minutes or till done. Cut slice from top of each. Scoop out insides; mash. Add sour cream, cream cheese, milk, butter or margarine, onion salt, and pepper; beat till smooth and fluffy. Stir in pimiento. Fill potato shells with mashed potato mixture. Return to oven and bake 15 minutes more or till hot. Makes 5 servings.

Dress up plain fresh or frozen vegetables for company with an herb butter. For each 3 or 4 servings of vegetable, combine about 2 tablespoons butter or margarine with ½ teaspoon herb or seed. Choose from these dried and crushed herbs: basil, marjoram, oregano, rosemary, savory or thyme; caraway seed; celery seed; fennel seed; or dried dillweed.

Another easy fix-up is to top your cooked vegetable with Easy Hollandaise Sauce (see recipe, page 31).

Or, sprinkle your favorite vegetable with grated Parmesan cheese, shredded cheddar cheese, or bacon bits.

Feature Linguine Romano *with roasted beef or pork, chicken, or baked ham. It's an easy side dish to prepare and provides an interesting change of pace from potatoes.*

LINGUINE ROMANO

4 ounces linguine, spaghetti, *or* noodles

2 3-ounce packages cream cheese, softened

1 tablespoon all-purpose flour

1 cup milk

⅓ cup grated romano *or* Parmesan cheese

¾ teaspoon dried thyme *or* basil, crushed

⅛ teaspoon pepper

1 2½-ounce jar sliced mushrooms, drained

Cook linguine, spaghetti, or noodles in large amount boiling salted water till done; drain. Meanwhile, in small saucepan stir cream cheese over low heat till soft; blend in flour. Stir in milk, cheese, thyme or basil, and pepper. Cook and stir over medium heat till mixture thickens and bubbles. Continue 1 to 2 minutes more. Stir in mushrooms; heat through. Add to drained linguine, tossing to coat evenly. Serve at once; pass additional romano *or* Parmesan cheese and pepper, if desired. Makes 4 to 6 servings.

SQUASH-APPLE BAKE

2 medium acorn *or* butternut squash (16 ounces each)

1 20-ounce can pie-sliced apples

2 tablespoons cornstarch

¾ cup dark corn syrup

2 tablespoons butter *or* margarine

1 teaspoon lemon juice

¾ teaspoon ground nutmeg

½ teaspoon salt

¼ cup chopped pecans

Halve and seed squash; place, cut side down, in shallow baking pan. Bake in 350° oven for 30 to 40 minutes or till barely tender (do not overcook). Cool slightly and peel. Cut into ½-inch slices. Drain apples, reserving liquid. Gently stir together apples and squash; turn into a 12x7½x2-inch baking dish. Stir together reserved apple liquid and cornstarch; stir in corn syrup, butter, lemon juice, nutmeg, and salt. Cook and stir till thickened and bubbly. Continue 1 to 2 minutes more. Pour over squash and apples. Sprinkle with nuts. Bake in 350° oven for 25 to 30 minutes. Serves 6.

PARMESAN OVEN RICE

3 tablespoons butter *or* margarine

⅔ cup long grain rice

1 13¾-ounce can (1⅔ cups) chicken broth

¼ cup grated Parmesan cheese

2 tablespoons snipped parsley

½ teaspoon salt

Dash pepper

In medium skillet melt butter or margarine over medium-low heat; add rice. Cook and stir till rice is coated and light golden brown. Remove from heat. Stir in chicken broth, cheese, parsley, salt, and pepper. Turn mixture into a 1-quart casserole. Bake, covered, in 350° oven for 50 minutes; stir after 30 minutes. Makes 4 servings.

ONION BUNS pictured on pages 38–39

1¼ cups finely chopped onion	¼ cup shortening
2 tablespoons butter *or* margarine	2 tablespoons sugar
	¾ teaspoon salt
2½ to 3 cups all-purpose flour	2 eggs
1 package active dry yeast	1 tablespoon milk
¾ cup milk	⅛ teaspoon salt

Cook onion in butter till tender but not brown. Remove 2 tablespoons mixture; set remainder aside. In large mixer bowl combine *1½ cups* of the flour and the yeast. In saucepan heat ¾ cup milk, shortening, sugar, and ¾ teaspoon salt just till warm (115° to 120°) and shortening is almost melted; stir constantly. Add to flour mixture; add *1 egg* and the 2 tablespoons onion mixture. Beat at low speed of electric mixer for ½ minute, scraping bowl. Beat 3 minutes at high speed. Stir in as much of the remaining flour as you can mix in with a spoon. Turn out onto lightly floured surface. Knead in enough of the remaining flour to make a moderately soft dough that is smooth and elastic (3 to 5 minutes total). Shape into a ball. Place in lightly greased bowl; turn once. Cover and let rise in a warm place till double (about 1¼ hours).

Beat remaining egg slightly; add *1 tablespoon* of the egg to remaining onion mixture. Stir 1 tablespoon milk and ⅛ teaspoon salt into onion mixture. Punch dough down; divide in half. Divide *each half* of dough into 6 portions. Cover; let rest 10 minutes. Shape into round buns. Place about 2 inches apart on a greased baking sheet. Make large indentation in center of each bun with fingers; spoon about *2 teaspoons* of the onion mixture into each indentation. Brush tops with remaining beaten egg. Sprinkle with poppy seeds, if desired. Cover; let rise till double (about 45 minutes). Bake in 375° oven for about 20 minutes. Makes 12 rolls.

Plain brown-and-serve rolls, refrigerated crescent rolls, and biscuits make easy breads for entertaining. Use a flavored butter to add a party touch.

For orange-flavored butter, combine ½ cup softened butter with 1 tablespoon powdered sugar, and ½ teaspoon finely shredded orange peel.

Make honey butter by combining ½ cup softened butter with ¼ cup honey and ½ teaspoon finely shredded lemon peel.

Green-flecked parsley butter is made by mixing ½ cup softened butter with 1 tablespoon snipped parsley; 1 teaspoon lemon juice; ¼ teaspoon dried savory, crushed; ⅛ teaspoon salt; and dash pepper.

Serve the flavored butters in small bowls. Or, mold and chill in fancy butter molds.

DILL COTTAGE CHEESE BREAD

2½ cups all-purpose flour	¼ cup water
1 package active dry yeast	2 tablespoons sugar
1 tablespoon finely chopped onion	2 tablespoons butter *or* margarine
2 teaspoons dillseed	1 teaspoon salt
1 cup cream-style cottage cheese	1 egg

In large mixer bowl combine *1½ cups* of the flour, yeast, onion, and dillseed. In saucepan heat cottage cheese, water, sugar, butter, and salt just till warm (115° to 120°) and butter is almost melted; stir constantly. Add to flour mixture; add egg. Beat at low speed of electric mixer for ½ minute, scraping bowl. Beat 3 minutes at high speed. By hand, stir in remaining flour. Cover; let rise till double, about 1 hour. Stir down. Spread evenly in greased 9x5x3-inch loaf pan. Cover; let rise till almost double (about 30 minutes). Bake in 350° oven 25 to 30 minutes. Remove from pan. If desired, brush with melted butter; sprinkle with additional dillseed. Makes 1 loaf.

Honey Swirl Coffee Cake
Cranberry Ladder Coffee Cake

HONEY SWIRL COFFEE CAKE

4½ to 4¾ cups all-purpose flour
2 packages active dry yeast
1 cup milk
½ cup sugar
½ cup butter *or* margarine
1 teaspoon salt
2 eggs
Raisin Filling

In large mixer bowl stir together *2 cups* of the flour and yeast. Heat and stir milk, sugar, butter, and salt till warm (115° to 120°). Add to flour mixture; add eggs. Beat at low speed of electric mixer ½ minute, scraping bowl. Beat 3 minutes at high speed. Stir in as much of the remaining flour as you can mix in with a spoon. Turn out onto lightly floured surface. Knead in enough remaining flour to make a moderately soft dough that is smooth and elastic (3 to 5 minutes total). Place in lightly greased bowl; turn once. Cover; let rise in warm place till double (1¼ to 1½ hours). Punch down; divide in half. Cover; let rest 10 minutes. On floured surface roll *each half* of dough to 14x8-inch rectangle. Spread *half* of Raisin Filling over *each* rectangle to within ½ inch of edges. Starting from long side, roll up jelly-roll fashion. Pinch edge to seal. Cut into 1-inch slices. Arrange slices, cut side down, in greased 10-inch tube pan, making 4 staggered layers. Cover; let rise till double (45 to 50 minutes). Bake in 350° oven 40 to 50 minutes. Let stand 10 minutes in pan. Invert onto rack; cool slightly. Makes 1.

Raisin Filling: Combine 1¼ cups *raisins,* ⅓ cup chopped *pecans,* ⅔ cup *honey,* ⅓ cup packed *brown sugar,* and 1 teaspoon ground *cinnamon.*

CRANBERRY LADDER COFFEE CAKE

3½ to 3¾ cups all-purpose flour
1 package active dry yeast
1 cup milk
⅓ cup sugar
¼ cup butter *or* margarine
1 teaspoon salt
1 egg
Cranberry Filling
Powdered Sugar Icing
Toasted sliced almonds

In large mixer bowl combine *2 cups* of the flour and yeast. Heat and stir milk, sugar, butter, and salt till warm (115° to 120°). Add to flour mixture; add egg. Beat at low speed of electric mixer ½ minute, scraping bowl. Beat 3 minutes at high speed. Stir in as much of the remaining flour as you can mix in with a spoon. Turn out onto lightly floured surface. Knead in enough of the remaining flour to make moderately stiff dough that is smooth and elastic (6 to 8 minutes total). Place in greased bowl; turn once. Cover; let rise till double (1 to 1¼ hours). Punch down; divide in half. Cover; let rest 10 minutes. On floured surface roll *each half* of dough to a 9-inch square. Place on greased baking sheets. Spread Cranberry Filling in 3-inch-wide strip down center of each square. With kitchen shears, snip sides toward center in strips 3 inches long and 1 inch wide. Fold strips over filling, alternating from side to side. Cover; let rise till double (30 to 45 minutes). Bake in 375° oven about 25 minutes. Cool slightly; top with Powdered Sugar Icing and almonds. Makes 2.

Cranberry Filling: In small bowl combine ¾ cup *cranberry-orange relish,* ¼ cup packed *brown sugar,* and 1 teaspoon ground *cinnamon.*

Powdered Sugar Icing: In small bowl combine 1 cup *powdered sugar,* ¼ teaspoon *vanilla,* and enough *milk* (about 1½ tablespoons) to make of drizzling consistency.

Offer both of these coffee cakes at a morning coffee or brunch. Serve them on a wooden pizza board, which will allow plenty of room for slicing and serving.

Bake the Honey Swirl Coffee Cake *a week or two in advance and freeze it. Simply cool completely on a wire rack, then wrap in foil and freeze. To serve, thaw the wrapped cake 3 or more hours at room temperature. Without unwrapping it, reheat in a 325° oven for 20 minutes.*

Follow the same instructions for freezing Cranberry Ladder Coffee Cake, *but do not add icing and almonds till cake is reheated.*

Banana-Orange Bread *baked in soup cans makes an unusual base for tea sandwiches. Make open-faced or closed sandwiches of cream cheese or peanut butter, then cut into halves or quarters.*

Garnish open-faced sandwiches with pecan halves, toasted coconut, or fresh fruit.

BANANA-ORANGE BREAD

1 cup sugar	½ cup whole wheat flour
½ cup cooking oil	½ cup unprocessed wheat bran
3 large ripe bananas, mashed (1½ cups)	2 teaspoons baking powder
	½ teaspoon baking soda
¼ cup orange marmalade	¼ teaspoon salt
2 beaten eggs	¼ cup chopped pecans
1 cup all-purpose flour	¼ cup flaked coconut

In mixing bowl combine sugar and oil; add bananas, orange marmalade, and eggs; mix well. Stir together flours, bran, baking powder, baking soda, and salt; stir into banana mixture. Stir in pecans and coconut. Divide batter into 5 clean, greased 10 to 11-ounce soup cans. Bake in 325° oven about 40 minutes or till done. (Or, pour batter into 2 greased 7½x3½x2-inch loaf pans. Bake in 325° oven about 55 minutes or till done.) Makes 5 small or 2 large loaves.

CREAM CHEESE BISCUITS

2 cups all-purpose flour	1 3-ounce package cream cheese
1 tablespoon baking powder	
½ teaspoon salt	⅔ cup milk
¼ cup butter *or* margarine	3 tablespoons raspberry jam

Stir together flour, baking powder, and salt. Cut in butter or margarine and cream cheese till mixture resembles coarse crumbs. Make a well in center. Add milk all at once. Stir just till dough clings together. Knead gently 4 or 5 strokes on lightly floured surface.

Roll or pat dough to slightly less than ½-inch thickness. Cut with floured 2-inch biscuit cutter. Place on ungreased baking sheet. Press down deep into center of each biscuit with thumb. Brush biscuits with additional *milk*. Spoon about ½ *teaspoon* of the jam into each indentation. Bake in 450° oven for 10 to 12 minutes. Makes 18.

CORN-RYE BISCUITS

1 cup all-purpose flour	½ teaspoon sugar
⅓ cup rye flour	½ teaspoon caraway seed
¼ cup cornmeal	¼ cup shortening
1 tablespoon baking powder	⅔ cup milk
½ teaspoon salt	Cornmeal

Stir together flours, ¼ cup cornmeal, baking powder, salt, sugar, and caraway seed. Cut in shortening till mixture resembles coarse crumbs. Make a well in the center; add milk all at once. Stir quickly with fork just till dough follows fork around bowl. Turn onto lightly floured surface (dough should be soft). Knead gently 10 to 12 strokes. Roll or pat dough to ½-inch thickness. Cut dough with a floured 2½-inch biscuit cutter. Dip tops and bottoms of biscuits in cornmeal. Place on greased baking sheet; bake in 450° oven 12 to 14 minutes. Makes 8.

WILD RICE MUFFINS

¼ cup wild rice	1 tablespoon brown sugar
2 cups water	½ teaspoon salt
½ teaspoon salt	¼ teaspoon ground sage
1 cup all-purpose flour	2 eggs
½ cup whole wheat flour	1 cup milk
1 tablespoon baking powder	⅓ cup cooking oil

Rinse rice in cold running water in a strainer for 1 to 2 minutes, lifting rice with fingers. In medium saucepan combine rice, 2 cups water, and ½ teaspoon salt; bring to boiling. Reduce heat; cover and simmer 45 minutes or till rice is tender. Drain and cool slightly.

Meanwhile, in mixing bowl stir together flours, baking powder, sugar, ½ teaspoon salt, and sage. Make a well in center. Combine eggs, milk, oil, and cooked rice. Add all at once to flour mixture. Stir quickly just till moistened (batter should be lumpy). Fill well-greased muffin cups ¾ full. Bake in 400° oven for 20 to 25 minutes. Makes 12 to 14.

MOLASSES CORN BREAD

1½ cups whole bran cereal	½ teaspoon salt
1 cup all-purpose flour	2 eggs
½ cup yellow cornmeal	1 cup milk
½ cup sugar	½ cup molasses
1 tablespoon baking powder	½ cup shortening

Stir together cereal, flour, cornmeal, sugar, baking powder, and salt. Add eggs, milk, molasses, and shortening. Beat with rotary beater just till blended; do not overbeat. Turn into greased 9x9x2-inch baking pan. Bake in 425° oven for 25 to 30 minutes. Serve warm. Makes 8 or 9 servings.

WHOLE WHEAT HONEY BREAD   pictured on page 38

1½ cups whole wheat flour	1¼ cups buttermilk or sour milk
⅔ cup all-purpose flour	⅓ cup honey
2 teaspoons baking powder	¼ cup butter or margarine,
½ teaspoon baking soda	melted
¾ teaspoon salt	½ cup chopped walnuts
1 beaten egg	½ cup raisins

In mixing bowl stir together the flours, baking powder, soda, and salt. Combine egg, buttermilk, honey, and butter; add to dry ingredients, stirring just till moistened. Fold in nuts and raisins. Turn into greased 8x4x2-inch loaf pan. Bake in 375° oven for 50 to 60 minutes or till done. Cool 10 minutes. Remove from pan; cool thoroughly. Wrap and store overnight. Makes 1 loaf.

If you can't serve muffins immediately after baking, tip them to one side in the pan to prevent crusts from becoming soggy. To reheat, wrap in foil and bake in 400° oven for 15 to 20 minutes.

DESSERTS

*Clockwise from top left: Strawberry-Cream Cheese Pie
(see recipe, page 62), Buttermilk Chocolate Cake
with Mocha Butter Frosting (see recipe, page 56),
Ambrosia (see recipe, page 64), Almond Thumbprints
(see recipe, page 66), and Lemon Cheesecake
(see recipe, page 63)*

Plan a dessert buffet for a large gathering. Have the guests bring their old-fashioned favorite such as this chocolate cake or any of the other sweets pictured on pages 54 and 55. Serve them on heirloom plates and dishes.

Borrow or rent old movies for entertainment, and offer prizes for the best vintage costumes worn by your guests.

BUTTERMILK CHOCOLATE CAKE pictured on pages 54–55

½ cup water	1 cup sugar
3 squares (3 ounces) unsweetened chocolate	½ cup packed brown sugar
	1 teaspoon vanilla
1¾ cups all-purpose flour	2 eggs
1 teaspoon baking soda	⅔ cup buttermilk or sour milk
¼ teaspoon salt	Mocha Butter Frosting
½ cup shortening	Chopped walnuts

Grease and lightly flour three 8x1½-inch round baking pans; set aside. In saucepan combine water and chocolate; stir over low heat till chocolate melts. Remove from heat; set aside. Stir together flour, soda, and salt. In mixer bowl beat shortening on medium speed of electric mixer about 30 seconds. Add sugars and vanilla; beat till well combined. Add eggs, one at a time, beating well after each. Stir in chocolate mixture. Add dry ingredients and buttermilk alternately to beaten mixture, beating on low speed after each addition till just combined. Turn batter into prepared pans. Bake in 350° oven for 20 to 25 minutes or till cakes test done. Cool 10 minutes in pans. Remove pans; cool well on racks. Frost and decorate with Mocha Butter Frosting; press nuts into sides. Serves 12.

Mocha Butter Frosting: In mixer bowl beat ½ cup *butter* with ⅓ cup unsweetened *cocoa powder* and 1½ teaspoons instant *coffee crystals* till light and fluffy. Gradually add *half* of 6¾ to 7¼ cups sifted *powdered sugar*, beating well. Beat in ⅓ cup *milk* and 2 teaspoons *vanilla*. Gradually beat in remaining powdered sugar. Beat in additional milk, if needed, to make frosting of spreading consistency.

SHERRIED FIG CAKE

1 cup dried figs	2 cups packaged biscuit mix
2 inches stick cinnamon	½ cup sugar
2 teaspoons finely shredded lemon peel	¼ teaspoon ground ginger
	1 egg
1 tablespoon lemon juice	1 tablespoon butter, softened
¼ cup sugar	1 teaspoon vanilla
¼ cup dry sherry	Sherry Icing

In saucepan combine figs, cinnamon, lemon peel and juice, and 1 cup *water*. Bring to boiling; reduce heat and simmer, covered, 30 minutes. Add the ¼ cup sugar and sherry; cook 5 minutes more. Remove from heat; cool. Drain figs, reserving ⅔ cup liquid. Chop figs.

In mixer bowl combine biscuit mix, ½ cup sugar, and the ginger; add reserved fig liquid, egg, butter, and vanilla. Beat on medium speed of electric mixer 4 minutes. Stir in figs. Turn batter into greased and floured 9-inch fluted tube pan. Bake in 350° oven 40 minutes or till done. Cool in pan 15 minutes. Invert onto rack; remove pan. When cool, drizzle with Sherry Icing.

Sherry Icing: Combine ½ cup sifted *powdered sugar* and enough dry *sherry* (about 2 teaspoons) to make of drizzling consistency.

COCONUT CAKE RING

⅓ cup dark corn syrup	1 package 2-layer-size regular white cake mix (no pudding)
¼ cup packed brown sugar	
¼ cup butter, melted	
⅔ cup shredded coconut	½ teaspoon almond extract

Combine corn syrup, brown sugar, and melted butter. Spread in bottom of a 5½-cup ring mold. Sprinkle with coconut. Mix cake according to package directions. Stir in almond extract. Using *3 cups* of the batter, fill the mold half full. (See sidebar for using remaining batter.) Bake in 350° oven for 30 minutes. Turn out onto serving plate immediately. Serve warm.

Use the extra cake batter to make 6 cupcakes; bake in a 350° oven for 20 minutes. They're terrific to pack in lunch boxes or to offer children at a party.

GREEK LEMON CAKE

1 package 2-layer-size regular lemon cake mix (no pudding)	½ cup cooking oil
	1 cup chopped walnuts
1 cup uncooked farina	1 cup sugar
1 cup milk	½ teaspoon finely shredded lemon peel
5 eggs	3 tablespoons lemon juice

Grease two 9x9x2-inch baking pans. In large mixer bowl combine cake mix and farina. Add milk, eggs, and oil. Beat at medium speed of electric mixer for amount of time given on cake mix package. Stir in ¾ *cup* of the nuts. Divide batter evenly between prepared pans. Bake in 350° oven 30 to 35 minutes or till cakes test done. Place on wire racks; do not remove from pans.

Meanwhile, in saucepan combine 1½ cups *water,* sugar, lemon peel, and lemon juice; bring to boiling. Boil gently, uncovered, for 10 minutes. With fork, prick holes in tops of hot cakes. Slowly spoon *half* of the hot syrup over *each* cake. Sprinkle with remaining nuts. Cool. Makes 2.

LEMON-FILBERT POUND CAKE

1 cup butter, softened	1 cup lemon yogurt
2¾ cups sugar	½ teaspoon vanilla
6 eggs	½ teaspoon finely shredded lemon peel
3 cups all-purpose flour	
½ teaspoon salt	½ cup chopped filberts
¼ teaspoon baking soda	Sifted powdered sugar

Grease and flour two 8x4x2-inch loaf pans. In large mixer bowl beat butter at medium speed of electric mixer till creamy and fluffy. Gradually add sugar, beating about 13 minutes or till fluffy and sugar is dissolved. Add eggs, one at a time, beating 1 minute after each; scrape bowl often. Beat 2 minutes more. Mix flour, salt, and soda. Combine yogurt, vanilla, and lemon peel. Add flour and yogurt mixtures alternately to creamed mixture; beat just till well blended. Fold in nuts. Divide batter evenly between prepared pans. Bake in 325° oven 1¼ to 1½ hours. Cool in pans 15 minutes; remove and cool on rack. Sprinkle with powdered sugar. Makes 2 loaves.

Freeze remaining Crepes *for another party. Stack* Crepes *with 2 sheets of waxed paper between each layer. Overwrap in foil and freeze. To use, let* Crepes *thaw at room temperature about 1 hour before filling.*

CRANANA CREPES À LA MODE

12 Crepes	1 tablespoon cornstarch
1 cup sugar	1 tablespoon cold water
¼ cup water	3 small bananas, sliced
1½ cups fresh *or* frozen	(1½ cups)
cranberries	Lemon sherbet

Prepare Crepes. In saucepan combine sugar and the ¼ cup water. Heat and stir till boiling and sugar dissolves. Stir in cranberries; cook about 5 minutes or till skins pop. Combine cornstarch with the 1 tablespoon cold water. Stir into cranberry mixture. Cook and stir till thickened and bubbly. Cook and stir 1 to 2 minutes more. Remove from heat; stir in bananas.

Spoon about *3 tablespoons* of the fruit mixture onto unbrowned side of *each* Crepe; fold over 2 opposite edges of Crepe so they overlap atop filling. Place on dessert plates; top each with small scoop of sherbet. Serves 12.

Crepes: In bowl combine 1¼ cups *milk,* 1 cup packaged *pancake mix,* 2 *eggs,* 1 tablespoon *sugar,* and 1 tablespoon *cooking oil;* beat with rotary beater till well blended. Heat a lightly greased 6-inch skillet. Remove from heat. Spoon in about *1½ tablespoons* batter; lift and tilt skillet to spread batter evenly. Return to heat; brown crepe on one side only. Invert pan over paper toweling; remove crepe. Repeat with remaining batter to make 24 crepes, greasing skillet occasionally.

APRICOT-ALMOND ROLLS

12 Crepes (see recipe, above)	¾ cup apricot preserves
½ cup whipping cream	¼ cup toasted slivered almonds
1 tablespoon apricot brandy	

Prepare Crepes. In mixing bowl combine whipping cream and brandy and beat till soft peaks form. Chill till serving time. Spread unbrowned side of each Crepe with *1 tablespoon* of the preserves; roll up Crepe. Place Crepes, seam side down, in 13x9x2-inch baking dish. Cover and bake in 375° oven for 15 minutes or till Crepes are heated through. To serve, place 2 Crepes on each dessert plate. Top with whipped cream mixture and almonds. Makes 6 servings.

Provide an assortment of dippers for Butterscotch Fondue. *Besides angel cake, use bite-size chunks of pound cake, apples, pears, and bananas for variety in taste and appearance.*

BUTTERSCOTCH FONDUE

½ cup butter *or* margarine	1 14-ounce can *sweetened condensed* milk
2 cups packed brown sugar	1 teaspoon vanilla
1 cup light corn syrup	Angel cake, cubed
2 tablespoons water	

In saucepan melt butter; stir in brown sugar, corn syrup, and water. Bring to boiling. Add sweetened condensed milk; simmer, stirring constantly, till mixture reaches 230° (thread stage). Add vanilla. Transfer to fondue pot; keep warm over fondue burner. If fondue becomes too thick, stir in a little *milk.* Spear cake cubes on fondue forks; swirl in fondue to coat. Makes 8 servings.

CLASSIC CARAMEL FLAN

½ cup sugar	4 eggs
3 cups milk	¼ teaspoon salt
4 inches stick cinnamon	½ cup sugar

Remember this dessert for an easy but elegant finish to almost any meal. It's traditional with Spanish or Mexican foods, but also sets off a salad or a soup meal with flair.

In skillet over medium heat melt ½ cup sugar, stirring constantly, till golden brown. Pour into 8-inch flan pan *or* 8x1½-inch round baking dish; quickly tilt to coat bottom. Heat milk and cinnamon till milk is warm (110° to 115°); cool slightly. Discard cinnamon. Beat eggs and salt; gradually add ½ cup sugar, beating well. Gradually stir in milk. Carefully pour mixture into caramel-coated dish. Set in a larger baking pan on oven rack. Add 1 inch *boiling water* to the large pan. Bake in 325° oven 45 minutes or till knife inserted off-center comes out clean; *center will be soft*. Chill. Loosen sides; invert onto serving platter. Makes 8 servings.

PINEAPPLE-ORANGE CREME

3 tablespoons sugar	¼ cup orange juice
1½ teaspoons all-purpose flour	1 slightly beaten egg
⅓ cup unsweetened pineapple juice	½ cup whipping cream

In small saucepan combine sugar and flour. Stir in pineapple juice and orange juice. Cook and stir over medium heat till thickened and bubbly. Gradually stir the hot mixture into the beaten egg. Return all to saucepan; cook and stir 1 to 2 minutes more. Cover and chill without stirring. Whip cream to soft peaks; fold into chilled mixture. Serve over cake, gingerbread, or fresh fruit. Makes about 1⅔ cups.

CHERRY BROWNIE PUDDING CAKE

¼ cup butter *or* margarine	½ teaspoon baking powder
1 cup sugar	½ teaspoon salt
½ teaspoon vanilla	2 egg whites
2 egg yolks	¼ cup water
1 21-ounce can cherry pie filling	2 tablespoons butter *or* margarine, melted
2 squares (2 ounces) unsweetened chocolate, melted and cooled	1 tablespoon lemon juice
1 cup all-purpose flour	Vanilla ice cream

In mixer bowl beat ¼ cup butter on medium speed of electric mixer about 30 seconds. Add sugar and vanilla; beat till well mixed. Add yolks; beat well. Stir in *1 cup* of the pie filling and the chocolate. Stir together flour, baking powder, and salt; add to chocolate mixture. Mix well.

Wash beaters well. Beat egg whites till stiff peaks form; fold into chocolate mixture. Stir water, melted butter, and lemon juice into remaining pie filling; spread in a 9x9x2-inch baking pan. Spoon batter over. Bake in 350° oven 40 minutes. Serve warm with ice cream. Makes 8 servings.

Charlotte Russe

CHARLOTTE RUSSE

12 ladyfingers, split	**1** cup dairy sour cream
2 envelopes unflavored gelatin	**2** teaspoons vanilla
¾ cup sugar	**4** egg whites
¼ teaspoon salt	**1** cup whipping cream
2 cups milk	Raspberry Sauce
4 slightly beaten egg yolks	

Line the sides of a 2-quart mold *or* soufflé dish with ladyfingers. Place 6 split ladyfingers spoke fashion in bottom of mold, trimming as necessary to fit. In medium saucepan combine gelatin, sugar, and salt. Stir in milk and yolks. Cook and stir over medium-low heat till mixture coats a metal spoon. Remove from heat; gradually stir into sour cream. Stir in vanilla. Chill till mixture mounds slightly.

Beat egg whites till stiff peaks form. Fold in gelatin mixture. Whip cream till soft peaks form; fold in. Spoon into lined mold. Chill several hours or overnight till firm. To serve, unmold on platter and drizzle with a little Raspberry Sauce. Garnish with fresh or frozen raspberries, if desired; pass remaining sauce. Makes 12 to 16 servings.

Raspberry Sauce: Thaw two 10-ounce packages frozen *red raspberries;* drain, reserving ½ cup syrup. In saucepan combine ¼ cup *sugar* and 4 teaspoons *cornstarch.* Stir in reserved syrup; cook and stir till thickened and bubbly. Cook and stir 1 to 2 minutes more. Cool slightly; stir in raspberries. Chill. Makes 1½ cups.

Let a spectacular dessert such as Charlotte Russe *serve as the centerpiece for a special meal. Here, the dessert is placed in a wicker basket, then decked with a wreath of greenery from the florist or your garden. Offer champagne with dessert.*

DOUBLE COFFEE SOUFFLÉ

¼ cup butter *or* margarine	**½** cup water
⅓ cup all-purpose flour	**6** egg yolks
2 teaspoons instant coffee	**6** egg whites
crystals	**¼** cup sugar
Dash salt	Coffee-Pecan Sauce
1 cup milk	

In small saucepan melt butter or margarine; stir in flour, coffee, and salt. Add milk and water all at once. Cook and stir till thickened and bubbly; remove from heat. In small mixer bowl beat yolks at high speed of electric mixer about 5 minutes or till thick and lemon-colored. Slowly add about *half* of coffee mixture to yolks, stirring constantly. Return all to coffee mixture in pan. Thoroughly wash beaters. In large mixer bowl beat egg whites at high speed of mixer till soft peaks form. Gradually add ¼ cup sugar, beating till stiff peaks form. Gently fold coffee mixture into egg whites. Pour into 2-quart soufflé dish with foil collar. Bake in 325° oven for 1¼ hours or till knife inserted halfway between center and edge comes out clean. Remove from oven; detach collar. Serve at once with Coffee-Pecan Sauce. Makes 6 to 8 servings.

Coffee-Pecan Sauce: In small saucepan stir together 4 teaspoons *cornstarch* and 2 teaspoons *instant coffee crystals.* Add ¾ cup *water* and ½ cup light *corn syrup;* cook and stir till thickened and bubbly. Stir in ¼ cup chopped *pecans,* 1 tablespoon *butter or margarine,* and 1 teaspoon *vanilla.* Serve warm. Makes 1¼ cups.

To make a foil collar for a soufflé dish, measure enough 12-inch-wide foil to go around the dish and overlap 1 inch. Fold foil in thirds lengthwise. Butter one side well; sprinkle with a little sugar. Wrap foil around the dish, buttered side in, extending collar 2 inches above the top edge. Secure collar with tape.

A day before the party, get a head start on your soufflé by preparing the collar. Then, prepare the soufflé mixture to the point where the egg yolks are thoroughly mixed into coffee mixture. Chill this mixture separately from the unbeaten egg whites. About 1½ hours before serving time, beat the egg whites and fold in the coffee mixture. Bake as directed.

The Coffee-Pecan Sauce may be made ahead and simply reheated before serving.

Cool Strawberry-Cream Cheese Pie *thoroughly, about 6 hours, before serving. To keep meringue from sticking to the cutting knife, dip knife in water before cutting into the pie. Repeat whenever meringue sticks.*

To store pie, insert wooden picks halfway into surface of meringue to hold wrap away from pie. Loosely cover with clear plastic wrap and refrigerate.

Meringue will be somewhat rubbery after chilling, so serve it the day it is made, if possible.

STRAWBERRY-CREAM CHEESE PIE pictured on pages 54–55

Pastry for Single-Crust Pie
⅔ cup sugar
3 tablespoons cornstarch
¼ teaspoon salt
2 cups milk
3 slightly beaten egg yolks
1 teaspoon vanilla

1 3-ounce package cream cheese, softened
1 10-ounce package frozen sliced strawberries, thawed
4 teaspoons cornstarch
Meringue

Prepare and roll out pastry. Line a 9-inch pie plate. Trim pastry to ½ inch beyond edge. Flute edge; prick pastry. Bake in 450° oven 10 to 12 minutes or till golden. Cool on rack.

In saucepan mix sugar, 3 tablespoons cornstarch, and salt. Gradually stir in milk. Cook and stir till bubbly; cook and stir 2 minutes more. Remove from heat. Gradually stir *1 cup* of the hot mixture into yolks. Return mixture to saucepan; return to gentle boil. Cook and stir 2 minutes more. Remove from heat; stir in vanilla. Stir in cream cheese till smooth. Pour into baked pastry shell. Cover surface with plastic wrap. Set aside to cool.

In saucepan combine strawberries and 4 teaspoons cornstarch. Cook and stir till thickened and bubbly. Cook and stir 2 minutes more. Remove from heat; cover surface with clear plastic wrap. Cool to room temperature. Spread over vanilla filling. Prepare Meringue; spread over strawberry layer and seal to edge. Bake in 350° oven 12 to 15 minutes or till golden. Cool; garnish with sliced strawberries, if desired. Makes 8 servings.

Pastry for Single-Crust Pie: In bowl combine 1¼ cups all-purpose *flour* and ½ teaspoon *salt*. Cut in ⅓ cup *shortening* till pieces resemble small peas. Sprinkle 3 to 4 tablespoons *cold water* over mixture, one tablespoon at a time; toss gently with a fork. Form dough into a ball.

Meringue: In mixer bowl beat 3 *egg whites*, ½ teaspoon *vanilla*, and ¼ teaspoon *cream of tartar* at medium speed of electric mixer for 1 minute or till soft peaks form. Gradually add 6 tablespoons *sugar*, beating at high speed till stiff peaks form. Immediately spread over pie, carefully sealing to edges.

FROZEN PUMPKIN PIE

1 cup cooked *or* canned pumpkin
⅓ cup packed brown sugar
1 teaspoon pumpkin pie spice

1 quart vanilla ice cream, softened
Coconut Crust
Whipped cream *or* whipped topping

Stir together the pumpkin, brown sugar, and pie spice. Stir into ice cream till well combined. Turn mixture into cooled Coconut Crust. Freeze overnight or till solid. Remove from freezer about 10 minutes before serving. Top with whipped cream or topping. Makes 8 servings.

Coconut Crust: Stir together 2 cups flaked *coconut* and 3 tablespoons *butter or margarine,* melted. Turn into 9-inch pie plate; press mixture onto bottom and sides to form a firm, even crust. Bake in 325° oven for 20 minutes or till coconut is golden. Cool thoroughly.

LEMON CHEESECAKE pictured on pages 54–55

1½ cups fine zwieback crumbs
⅓ cup sugar
¾ teaspoon ground cinnamon
¼ teaspoon ground nutmeg
6 tablespoons butter *or* margarine, melted
¾ cup sugar
2 envelopes unflavored gelatin
¼ teaspoon salt
1 5⅓-ounce can (⅔ cup) evaporated milk
2 beaten egg yolks

1 teaspoon finely shredded lemon peel
2 12-ounce cartons (3 cups) cream-style cottage cheese
2 tablespoons lemon juice
1 teaspoon vanilla
2 egg whites
¼ cup sugar
1 cup whipping cream
Lemon twists (optional)
Fresh mint leaves (optional)

Process the cottage cheese in your blender till it's smooth, otherwise your cheesecake will have a lumpy texture. If you don't have a blender, press cottage cheese through a sieve to remove most of the lumps.

Mix crumbs, ⅓ cup sugar, and spices. Add butter, stirring till combined; reserve ¼ cup crumb mixture. Press remainder on bottom and 2½ inches up sides of 8-inch (*or* 2 inches up sides of 9-inch) springform pan. Chill.

For filling, in saucepan combine the ¾ cup sugar, gelatin, and salt. Stir in evaporated milk, then egg yolks. Cook and stir over low heat till mixture just boils and gelatin dissolves. Stir in lemon peel. Pour into large bowl; cool to room temperature.

Meanwhile, put cottage cheese in blender container, *half* at a time, and blend till smooth. Stir cottage cheese, lemon juice, and vanilla into gelatin mixture. Chill, stirring occasionally, till mixture mounds. Beat egg whites till soft peaks form; gradually add ¼ cup sugar, beating till stiff peaks form. Fold into gelatin mixture. Beat cream till soft peaks form; fold into gelatin mixture. Turn into chilled crust; sprinkle with reserved crumbs. Chill several hours or overnight. Garnish with lemon twists and mint leaves, if desired. Makes 10 to 12 servings.

FROZEN MOCHA MOUSSE

4 egg whites
⅔ cup sugar
1 cup chopped walnuts
¼ cup light corn syrup
1 tablespoon instant coffee crystals
1 tablespoon water

½ cup semisweet chocolate pieces
⅔ cup *sweetened condensed* milk
1 cup whipping cream
1 teaspoon vanilla
Chocolate curls

For meringue crust, beat egg whites till soft peaks form. Gradually add sugar, beating till stiff peaks form. Fold in nuts. Spread over bottom and sides of well-buttered and floured 9-inch pie plate, forming a high edge. Bake in 275° oven for 1 hour. Turn off oven; let meringue crust cool in oven with door closed for 2 hours.

For filling, mix corn syrup, coffee, and water; heat to boiling. Reduce heat; add chocolate and stir till melted. Remove from heat; stir in milk. Slowly stir in cream and vanilla. Cover; chill. Beat filling mixture till soft peaks form. Spoon into meringue crust. Cover; freeze several hours or overnight. Top with chocolate curls. Makes 8 servings.

Use any of the following fruits alone or in combination in Fruit Flambé: *sliced bananas or nectarines; peeled, sliced peaches, apricots, kiwi fruit, or mangoes; whole blueberries, raspberries, strawberries, or cherries; or fresh pineapple chunks.*

Tie brightly colored ribbons around an assortment of inexpensive stemmed dishes for serving dessert at your next party. Then let your guests take home the dishes as party favors.

FRUIT FLAMBÉ

¼ **cup butter** *or* **margarine**	¼ **cup orange juice**
½ **cup packed brown sugar**	3 **cups fruit (see sidebar)**
¼ **cup chopped pecans** *or*	¼ **cup light rum**
toasted, slivered almonds	**Vanilla ice cream**
½ **teaspoon ground cinnamon**	

In a 10-inch skillet *or* blazer pan of chafing dish melt butter or margarine; stir in sugar, nuts, and cinnamon. Add orange juice; cook and stir till bubbly. Add fruit; cook 1 to 2 minutes, stirring often, just till fruit is heated through. Sprinkle with *2 tablespoons* of the rum. Heat remaining 2 tablespoons rum just till warm in large ladle or small saucepan. Ignite rum with match and pour over fruit. Serve immediately over ice cream. Makes 6 servings.

AMBROSIA   pictured on pages 54–55

1 **15½-ounce can pineapple**	1 **cup seedless green grapes** *or*
chunks	**halved, seeded Emperor**
1 **medium banana, bias-sliced**	**grapes**
3 **medium oranges, peeled and**	½ **cup flaked coconut**
sectioned	½ **cup ginger ale (optional)**

Drain pineapple, reserving syrup. Dip banana slices in reserved pineapple syrup. Arrange *half* of each of the fruits in a 5-cup glass bowl. Sprinkle with *half* of the coconut. Arrange remaining fruits atop. Pour reserved pineapple syrup over all. Cover and chill. At serving time, pour ginger ale over fruits, if desired. Sprinkle with remaining coconut. Makes 4 to 6 servings.

The whipped cream and egg white topping in Strawberries Romanoff *is best when made shortly before serving. But you can make it several hours early and chill, if you wish. Stir before spooning atop the berries.*

STRAWBERRIES ROMANOFF

1 **quart fresh strawberries**	**Dash salt**
¼ **cup orange liqueur**	**Dash cream of tartar**
2 **tablespoons sugar**	1 **tablespoon sugar**
1 **egg white**	½ **cup whipping cream**
½ **teaspoon vanilla**	

Wash and hull strawberries; reserve 6 berries for garnish. Slice remaining berries; sprinkle with liqueur and 2 tablespoons sugar. Chill thoroughly. Beat egg white with vanilla, salt, and cream of tartar to soft peaks; add 1 tablespoon sugar and continue beating till stiff peaks form. Beat whipping cream till soft peaks form. Fold whipped cream into egg white. Spoon berries into dessert dishes or small bowls; top each serving with whipped cream mixture and garnish with a whole berry. Makes 6 servings.

Blueberries or Raspberries Romanoff: Prepare Strawberries Romanoff as above, *except* substitute fresh *blueberries or raspberries* for the strawberries; do not slice berries.

Fruit Flambé

For a decorative plate of cookies from just one dough, use a variety of preserves in Almond Thumbprints: *raspberry, cherry, apricot, strawberry, and pineapple.*

ALMOND THUMBPRINTS pictured on pages 54–55

1 cup butter *or* margarine, softened	¾ teaspoon almond extract
1 3-ounce package cream cheese, softened	2½ cups all-purpose flour
1 cup sugar	½ teaspoon baking soda
1 egg	¼ teaspoon salt
	1 cup finely chopped almonds
	½ cup fruit preserves

Beat together butter and cheese; beat in sugar, egg, and almond extract. Stir together flour, soda, and salt; stir into beaten mixture. Chill at least 1 hour. Shape into 1-inch balls; roll in almonds to coat. Place on ungreased cookie sheet. Make indentation in each by pressing with your thumb. Fill *each* with about ½ *teaspoon* of the preserves. Bake in 350° oven for 10 to 12 minutes or till golden. Cool on wire racks. Makes 48.

APRICOT-SPICE BARS

1 8-ounce package dried apricots, snipped	1 teaspoon baking powder
¾ cup water	¼ teaspoon salt
1½ cups all-purpose flour	3 slightly beaten eggs
½ cup sugar	1 cup packed brown sugar
¾ cup butter *or* margarine	1 teaspoon vanilla
¾ cup all-purpose flour	1 cup chopped almonds *or* pecans
2 teaspoons ground cinnamon	Sifted powdered sugar

In saucepan simmer apricots in the water, covered, 5 minutes. Set aside to cool. Combine the 1½ cups flour and sugar. Cut in butter till crumbly. Pat evenly into 13x9x2-inch baking pan. Bake in 350° oven 17 minutes. Meanwhile, combine the remaining ¾ cup flour, the cinnamon, baking powder, and salt. Combine eggs, brown sugar, and vanilla; add to flour mixture and mix well. Stir in undrained apricots and nuts. Spread over baked layer. Bake in 350° oven for 30 minutes or till top is set. Cool in pan on wire rack; sprinkle with powdered sugar. Cut into bars. Makes 48.

LEMONUT BARS

1 14-ounce can *sweetened condensed* milk	½ cup packed brown sugar
½ teaspoon finely shredded lemon peel	½ cup butter, softened
⅓ cup lemon juice	1½ cups whole wheat flour
	½ cup chopped walnuts
	1 teaspoon baking powder

Combine canned milk, lemon peel, and lemon juice; set aside. Beat together brown sugar and butter. Stir together flour, nuts, baking powder, and ½ teaspoon *salt;* stir into beaten mixture till crumbly. Reserve *1 cup* crumbs; pat remainder in bottom of greased 12x7½x2-inch baking dish. Spread lemon mixture over; sprinkle with reserved crumbs. Bake in 325° oven 30 to 35 minutes. Loosen edges. Cool; then chill. Cut into bars. Makes 24.

COFFEE-CHOCOLATE CHIP BARS

¾ cup packed brown sugar	1¼ cups all-purpose flour
½ cup butter *or* margarine	½ teaspoon baking soda
1 egg	½ teaspoon salt
1 tablespoon instant coffee crystals	1 6-ounce package semisweet chocolate pieces
½ teaspoon vanilla	¾ cup chopped walnuts

In mixer bowl beat together brown sugar and butter; beat in egg, coffee crystals, and vanilla. Stir together flour, soda, and salt; stir into butter mixture. Stir in chocolate pieces and nuts. Spread in greased 9x9x2-inch pan. Bake in 375° oven about 20 minutes. Cool; sprinkle with powdered sugar, if desired. Cut into squares. Makes 16.

GINGER-PEACH SHERBET

1¼ cups sugar	2 cups peach nectar
1 3-ounce package peach-flavored gelatin	2 cups ginger ale
	¼ cup lemon juice

In saucepan stir 2 cups *water* into sugar and gelatin. Heat and stir till sugar and gelatin dissolve completely. Cool to room temperature. Add nectar, ginger ale, and lemon juice. Freeze in a 5-quart ice cream freezer according to manufacturer's directions. Makes 16 to 20 servings.

CHOCOLATE-NUT SHERBET

2 eggs	¼ cup light corn syrup
⅔ cup sugar	¼ cup chocolate-flavored syrup
2 cups milk	½ cup chopped walnuts

Beat eggs at high speed of electric mixer till thick and lemon-colored. Gradually add sugar, beating till thick. Stir in milk, corn syrup, and chocolate syrup. Pour into an 8x8x2-inch pan; freeze firm. Break chunks into chilled mixer bowl; beat smooth. Stir in walnuts. Immediately return to cold pan. Freeze till firm again. Makes 8 to 10 servings.

CIDER ICE

2 cups apple juice *or* cider	½ cup orange juice
½ cup sugar	¼ cup lemon juice

In saucepan combine apple juice or cider and sugar; simmer 5 minutes. Cool. Add orange and lemon juices. Pour into 8x8x2-inch pan; freeze till firm. Break ice into chunks with spoon; turn into chilled mixer bowl and beat till fluffy. Return to cold pan. Freeze till firm again. Spoon into sherbet dishes. Serve immediately. Makes 6 servings.

During the Christmas season, host a cookie exchange. Each guest bakes a large batch of favorite holiday cookies to bring. Once there, divide the cookies so each guest takes home an assortment of goodies that would have taken days to prepare. Provide coffee and punch to drink with a sample of the treats.

SNACKS & BEVERAGES

*Clockwise from top left: Sangria
(see recipe, page 86), Deviled Nuts (see recipe,
page 76), Frozen Margarita (see recipe, page 89),
Chili con Queso (see recipe, page 78), Avocado Dip
(see recipe, page 77), Nachos (see recipe, page 71),
and Ham-Stuffed Tortilla Snacks (see recipe, page 70)*

ITALIAN PIZZA SNACKS

Keep snacks on hand such as
Italian Pizza Snacks or Mexicali
Pizza Snacks (pictured on pages
68–69) to serve to unexpected
guests. *Prepare the meat-sauce
mixture and spread over the
toasted muffins or bread slices,
but do not broil. Arrange on a baking sheet so the edges do not
touch. Freeze till solid. Remove
from freezer and transfer them to
moisture-vaporproof freezer bags
or containers and seal. Label and
return to freezer.*

*To serve, place frozen snacks on
a baking sheet. Bake in 400° oven
for 10 minutes; sprinkle with
shredded cheese and bake 5 minutes more.*

*Accompany the pizza snacks
with mugs of cold beer or iced tea.*

½ pound bulk Italian sausage,
  bulk pork sausage, or
  ground beef
¼ cup chopped onion
1 8-ounce can tomato sauce
½ teaspoon dried basil, crushed
½ teaspoon dried oregano,
  crushed
¼ teaspoon salt

4 English muffins, split and
  toasted or 8 slices French
  bread, toasted
1 small green pepper, thinly
  sliced or ½ cup sliced green
  olives
1 cup shredded mozzarella or
  provolone cheese

In skillet cook sausage or beef with onion till meat is browned; drain off fat.
Stir in tomato sauce, basil, oregano, and salt; cover and simmer about 10
minutes. Spread toasted muffin halves or bread slices with meat mixture; top
each with a green pepper ring or sliced green olives. Sprinkle with cheese.
Place muffins on baking sheet. Broil 4 inches from heat for 3 minutes or till
cheese melts. Makes 8.

Mexicali Pizza Snacks: Prepare Italian Pizza Snacks as directed above,
except omit basil, oregano, green pepper or olives, and mozzarella or provolone cheese. Stir ½ cup sliced pitted *ripe olives;* ½ of a 4-ounce can green
chili peppers, rinsed, seeded, and chopped; and ½ teaspoon dried *parsley
flakes* into meat mixture. Continue as directed. Sprinkle with 1 cup shredded
cheddar or Monterey Jack cheese. Broil as directed. Top each with a thin slice
of *tomato* and *shredded lettuce,* if desired.

HAM-STUFFED TORTILLA SNACKS   pictured on pages 68–69

12 6- to 8-inch flour tortillas
1½ cups finely chopped fully
  cooked ham
1 large apple, cored, peeled,
  and finely chopped
½ cup finely chopped celery

½ cup finely chopped chutney
1 egg yolk
1 egg white
2 teaspoons water
  Cooking oil for deep-fat
  frying

Stack tortillas; wrap in foil and place on baking sheet. Heat in 350° oven for 15
minutes or till warm and pliable. Meanwhile, to prepare filling, in bowl
combine ham, apple, celery, chutney, and egg yolk.

To assemble, work with one tortilla at a time (keep others warm in oven till
used). Spoon ¼ *cup* of the filling on left half of tortilla, spreading to within 1
inch of edge. Combine egg white and water; brush some over surface of
tortilla. Fold left edge up and over filling just till mixture is covered. Fold in
top and bottom sides envelope-fashion, then roll up to make a rectangular
shaped bundle. Moisten overlapping edges with egg white mixture to seal; lay
seam side down and set aside. Fill and fold remaining tortillas.

In saucepan heat 1½ inches cooking oil to 375°. Fry bundles, two at a time,
for 1 to 2 minutes or till golden brown, turning once. Drain on paper toweling.
Cut in half to serve. Serve warm. Makes 24 snacks.

NACHOS pictured on pages 68–69

Tortilla chips *or* large corn
  chips
Monterey Jack *or* cheddar
  cheese

Canned green chili peppers *or*
  jalapeño peppers, rinsed
  and seeded

Spread tortilla chips in a single layer on ovenproof plate or foil-lined baking sheet. Cut cheese into ¾ x ¾ x ¼-inch pieces. Cut peppers into thin strips, about ¾ inch long. Place a piece of cheese on each chip; top with a strip of chili. Bake in 400° oven for 5 minutes or till cheese melts. Serve hot.

LAMB BITES WITH YOGURT SAUCE

1 beaten egg
2 tablespoons milk
1 cup soft bread crumbs
2 tablespoons finely chopped
  onion
1 teaspoon seasoned salt

½ teaspoon dried tarragon,
  crushed
1 pound ground lamb *or* beef
½ cup plain yogurt
¼ cup finely chopped cucumber
1 tablespoon snipped parsley

For meatballs, in mixing bowl combine egg, milk, crumbs, onion, ¾ *teaspoon* of the seasoned salt, and tarragon. Add meat; mix well. Shape into 1-inch meatballs; place in shallow baking pan. Bake in 350° oven 15 to 18 minutes or till done. Drain on paper toweling. Meanwhile, combine yogurt, cucumber, parsley, and remaining ¼ teaspoon seasoned salt. Serve meatballs hot with wooden picks. Dip into yogurt mixture. Makes about 42 meatballs.

  Microwave cooking directions: Prepare meatballs as directed above. Arrange ⅓ at a time in a ring on a plate lined with paper toweling. Cover with paper toweling. Cook in countertop microwave oven on high power 3 minutes; turn plate once. Drain and serve as above.

SMOKY SAUSAGE CRESCENTS

1 3-ounce package cream
  cheese with chives
2 teaspoons Dijon-style
  mustard
1 teaspoon prepared
  horseradish

1 package (8) refrigerated
  crescent rolls
1 5-ounce package (16) small
  smoked sausage links

Soften cream cheese. In mixer bowl beat cream cheese on medium speed of electric mixer about 2 minutes. Add mustard and horseradish; beat till fluffy. Separate roll dough into triangles; cut each triangle in half to make 16 smaller triangles. Spread the first 2 inches of base of each triangle with *1 teaspoon* of the cream cheese mixture; add a sausage. Beginning with base, roll dough around the sausage. Place seam side down on greased baking sheet. Bake in 400° oven for 10 to 12 minutes. Makes 16.

With a little extra effort you can make Nachos *into an even better party food by preparing "home-made" tortilla chips. Stack store purchased corn or flour tortillas; cut stack into 6 wedges. In a heavy saucepan heat ½ inch cooking oil. Fry tortilla wedges, a few at a time, about 1 minute for corn tortillas or 45 seconds for flour tortillas or till lightly browned. Drain on paper toweling. Salt lightly, if desired. Prepare tortilla chips as directed in the* Nachos *recipe, and you've got the beginnings of a great party.*

APPETIZER PUFFS

1 stick pie crust mix	**Chicken Filling** *or*
2 eggs	**Tuna-Olive Filling**

In saucepan heat ⅔ cup *water* to boiling. Crumble pie crust mix; add to boiling water all at once. Stir vigorously over low heat till dough forms a ball. Cook and stir 1 minute; remove from heat. Add eggs; beat vigorously for 2 minutes. Drop dough by rounded teaspoonfuls onto ungreased baking sheet. Bake in 425° oven 20 to 25 minutes or till puffed, golden, and dry. Cool on wire rack. Split puffs; remove inside webbing. To serve, fill with Chicken or Tuna-Olive Filling. Makes about 40.

Chicken Filling: Combine 1 cup finely chopped *cooked chicken,* ¼ cup *mayonnaise or salad dressing,* 2 tablespoons finely chopped *celery,* 1 tablespoon chopped *pimiento,* 1 tablespoon dry *white wine or water,* ⅛ teaspoon *salt,* and dash *pepper.* Cover; chill. Makes 1¼ cups.

Tuna-Olive Filling: Combine one 6½-ounce can *tuna,* drained and flaked; ¼ cup chopped pimiento-stuffed *olives;* ¼ cup chopped fresh *mushrooms;* ¼ cup *mayonnaise or salad dressing;* 2 tablespoons grated *Parmesan cheese;* and 2 teaspoons prepared *mustard.* Cover and chill. Makes 1⅓ cups.

STUFFED APPLE WEDGES pictured on page 75

1 3-ounce package cream cheese	**¼ cup chopped walnuts *or* peanuts**
½ cup shredded Swiss *or* cheddar cheese (2 ounces)	**6 apples *or* pears** **2 tablespoons lemon juice** **2 tablespoons water**

Bring cheeses to room temperature. Beat cheeses together till well blended. Stir in nuts. Chill till needed. Cut each pear or apple in half lengthwise. With knife tip, remove stem ends. With melon baller, remove center of core. Fill hole with cheese mixture; flatten so filling will be even with cut surface of fruit. Place cut side down on board; with sharp knife, cut each half into 4 wedges. Combine lemon juice and water; brush over cut surfaces of fruit to prevent browning. Makes 48.

CHEESE-STUFFED MUSHROOMS

24 to 30 large fresh mushrooms	**½ of a 0.7- to 0.9-ounce envelope blue cheese salad dressing mix**
2 3-ounce packages cream cheese, softened	**¼ cup finely chopped walnuts**

Remove stems from mushrooms; reserve. Simmer mushroom caps and stems in boiling water for 2 minutes. Drain; invert caps on paper toweling. Cool. Chop enough stems to make ½ cup (save remainder for another use). Combine cheese and dry dressing mix; stir in nuts and chopped stems. Spoon into caps; place in shallow baking pan. Sprinkle with paprika, if desired. Bake in 425° oven 6 to 8 minutes. Makes 24 to 30.

When planning an afternoon reception, a cocktail party, or a noon luncheon, don't overlook the idea of serving an unusual sandwich. *The* Chicken Filling *and* Tuna-Olive Filling *for* Appetizer Puffs *make teriffic sandwich spreads for any of these informal get-togethers.*

Reception—*spread the chicken or tuna filling between two slices of white or whole wheat bread, then cut into fingers or triangles to make tea sandwiches. Or, cut fancy shapes from the sliced bread before spreading with filling.*

Cocktail Party—*spread the sandwich filling on party rye bread or crackers; top with a slice of olive, pimiento, or cucumber.*

Noon Luncheon—*serve the filling on toasted bread or pile it into a split onion roll. Add lettuce and tomato slices for a change from ordinary fare.*

SESAME CRISPS

1 cup all-purpose flour	2 tablespoons milk
½ teaspoon celery salt	1 slightly beaten egg white
¼ teaspoon garlic salt	2 tablespoons sesame seed
¼ cup cooking oil	

In small bowl combine flour, celery salt, and garlic salt. Add oil and milk all at once; stir with fork till well mixed. Form into a ball. Place between 2 sheets of waxed paper. Roll out to a 10-inch square; remove paper. Brush with egg white. Sprinkle with sesame seed; press in lightly with rolling pin. Cut into 2-inch squares or diamonds. Transfer to an ungreased baking sheet. Bake in 450° oven about 8 minutes or till lightly browned. Serve warm or cold. Makes 25 crackers.

Sesame Crisps are a good snack any time of day. Make them ahead to serve whenever friends or unexpected guests drop by.

To reheat in the microwave oven, arrange crackers in a ring on a plate. Heat on high power in countertop microwave oven for about 30 seconds.

ITALIAN CHEESE STICKS

6 tablespoons butter *or* margarine	½ teaspoon dried oregano, crushed
1 cup shredded sharp cheddar cheese (4 ounces)	¼ teaspoon salt
	Few dashes cayenne
1 cup all-purpose flour	2 tablespoons water

Bring butter and cheese to room temperature. Beat together the butter and cheese till well blended. Combine flour, oregano, salt, and cayenne; add to cheese mixture gradually. Add water; mix till well blended. Form dough into a ball. Roll out on floured surface to ¼-inch thickness. Cut into 3x¾-inch strips or cut into shapes with small cookie cutters. Bake on ungreased baking sheet in 400° oven for 8 to 10 minutes or till lightly browned. Serve warm or cold. Makes about 40.

RUMAKI

9 slices bacon, halved crosswise	¼ cup soy sauce
9 chicken livers, halved	1 tablespoon sugar
9 water chestnuts, halved	⅛ teaspoon ground ginger

Partially cook bacon; drain on paper toweling. Combine chicken livers and water chestnuts with the soy sauce, sugar, and ginger. Marinate about 20 minutes, stirring occasionally; drain.

Wrap 1 liver half and 1 water chestnut half in a half-slice of bacon; repeat with remaining. Secure with wooden picks. Place in 8x8x2-inch baking pan; bake in 450° oven for 10 to 12 minutes or till bacon is crisp. Makes 18.

Pineapple-Mushroom Rumaki: Prepare Rumaki as above, *except* substitute 9 fresh or canned *mushrooms,* halved, and 18 fresh or canned *pineapple chunks* for the chicken livers and water chestnuts.

Raid the toy box for different serving pieces when you have an adult party. These toys are especially appropriate when you're celebrating a new baby, back-to-school, Christmas, or a birthday. Offer hot appetizers in microwave-safe containers so they can be refilled and reheated as needed.

SALMON PASTRIES

1 7¾-ounce can salmon
2 beaten eggs
1 cup cream-style cottage cheese, drained
½ cup finely chopped cucumber

1 teaspoon dried dillweed
¼ teaspoon lemon pepper
½ of a 16-ounce package phyllo dough
¾ cup butter, melted

Drain salmon; flake, removing bones and skin. Combine with eggs, cheese, cucumber, dillweed, and lemon pepper. Unfold phyllo dough; spread 1 sheet flat. Brush with some butter. Top with second sheet; brush with butter. Add third sheet; brush with butter. Cut stack lengthwise into 2-inch strips. Place 1 scant tablespoon salmon mixture near end of each strip. Fold end over filling at 45 degree angle. Continue folding to form a triangle that encloses the filling, using entire strip of 3 layers. Repeat with remaining dough and filling. Place on baking sheet; brush with butter. Bake in 375° oven 18 minutes. Serve warm or cool. Makes 32.

You can have Glazed Meatballs ready in a matter of minutes if you freeze the meatballs in advance.

Shape and bake the meatballs as directed in the recipe, then wrap securely and freeze. When you need them, prepare the catsup-soy mixture. Heat the frozen meatballs directly in the sauce. Nothing could be easier, unless, it's serving ham cubes with the sauce from Glazed Meatballs (see photo at right). Cut fully-cooked ham into bite-size pieces, heat, and serve, just like the meatballs.

GLAZED MEATBALLS

3 slices bread
⅔ cup milk
2 slightly beaten eggs
1 tablespoon prepared horseradish
1½ pounds ground beef

½ cup catsup
¼ cup maple-flavored syrup
¼ cup water
¼ cup soy sauce
1 teaspoon ground allspice
½ teaspoon dry mustard

Soak bread in milk till soft. Add eggs, horseradish, 1 teaspoon *salt,* and ¼ teaspoon *pepper;* beat smooth. Add beef; mix well. Shape into ¾-inch meatballs; place on rack in shallow baking pan. Bake in 450° oven 10 to 15 minutes. Heat remaining ingredients to boiling; stir often. Add meatballs; heat through. Keep warm; serve with wooden picks. Makes 65.

SWEET-SOUR APPETIZER KEBABS

1 15¼-ounce can pineapple chunks (juice pack)
3 tablespoons brown sugar
1 tablespoon cornstarch
3 tablespoons vinegar
3 tablespoons soy sauce

20 cocktail franks *or* 5 frankfurters, quartered
1 large green pepper, cut into 1-inch pieces
1 8-ounce can water chestnuts, drained (optional)

Drain pineapple, reserving juice. In saucepan mix brown sugar and cornstarch. Slowly add reserved juice, vinegar, and soy; cook and stir till thick and bubbly. Cook and stir 1 to 2 minutes more. On short skewers thread pineapple chunks, franks, pepper squares, and water chestnuts, if desired. Place on rack in broiler pan; broil 4 to 5 inches from the heat 8 to 10 minutes. (*Or,* cook on grill over *medium* coals 10 to 12 minutes.) Turn once and baste with soy mixture. Heat remaining sauce for dipping. Makes 20.

*Stuffed Apple Wedges
(see recipe, page 72), Sweet-Sour Appetizer
Kebabs, Salmon Pastries, and Glazed Meatballs*

Cocktails Outdoors

Grilled Shrimp and Scallops*

Spicy Snacks*

Avocado Dip*

Vegetable Dippers

Assorted Crackers

Serve-Yourself Bar Drinks

Stage your next cocktail party outdoors with the sunset as backdrop and your garden as centerpiece.

Set up a bar in the backyard with plenty of buckets of ice. Let guests serve themselves. Plastic glasses and paper plates are appropriate for the informal setting, but feel free to use even your best crystal and china if you like.

Prepare the snack mix well ahead of the party. Cut up vegetable dippers and prepare the dip about 1 hour before guests arrive. Thread the marinated seafood and mushrooms on skewers before the party, then let guests cook their own over your hibachi or grill. They'll be swapping recipes and conversation in no time. Serves 12.

*See index for recipe pages.

GRILLED SHRIMP AND SCALLOPS

½ pound fresh *or* frozen medium shrimp in shells
½ pound fresh *or* frozen scallops
4 ounces whole fresh mushrooms
¼ cup cooking oil
2 tablespoons lemon juice
1 clove garlic, minced
1 teaspoon dried oregano, crushed
½ teaspoon salt
Lemon wedges

Thaw shrimp and scallops, if frozen. Peel and devein shrimp, leaving tails attached. Halve any large scallops. Place shrimp, scallops, and mushrooms in a deep bowl. For marinade, mix oil, lemon juice, garlic, oregano, and salt; pour over shrimp and scallops. Cover and marinate in refrigerator for 4 to 6 hours or overnight, stirring occasionally. Drain well, reserving marinade.

To grill: Place seafood and mushrooms in a greased wire grill basket or thread on short skewers. Grill over *hot* coals for 5 to 10 minutes or till seafood is done; turn and baste often with marinade.

To broil: Thread seafood and mushrooms on short skewers; place on rack in broiler pan. Broil 4 inches from heat for 3 to 5 minutes; turn and baste with marinade. Broil 3 to 5 minutes longer or till done.

Pass lemon wedges. Makes 12 servings.

DEVILED NUTS pictured on pages 68–69

¼ cup butter *or* margarine
1 tablespoon Worcestershire sauce
1 teaspoon chili powder
Dash bottled hot pepper sauce
1 pound unsalted roasted peanuts *or* pecans

In large skillet melt butter or margarine; stir in Worcestershire sauce, chili powder, and pepper sauce. Stir in nuts; cook over medium heat, stirring occasionally, about 25 minutes or till brown. (Nuts will become crisp when cool.) Drain on paper toweling; cool. Makes 3 cups.

SPICY SNACKS

1 egg white
2 teaspoons water
3 tablespoons sugar
¾ teaspoon ground cinnamon
⅛ teaspoon ground nutmeg
⅛ teaspoon ground ginger
5 cups bite-size shredded corn, wheat, *or* rice squares
1 9-ounce jar dry roasted peanuts

Combine egg white and water; stir in sugar, cinnamon, nutmeg, and ginger. Beat till frothy. In 13x9x2-inch baking pan mix cereal and nuts. Add egg white mixture; toss to coat. Bake in 350° oven for 15 minutes. Cool 5 minutes. Remove from pan; cool. Store in tightly covered container. Makes 7 cups.

AVOCADO DIP pictured on pages 68–69

1 large ripe avocado, peeled and seeded	¼ teaspoon salt
½ cup dairy sour cream	2 slices bacon, crisp-cooked, drained, and crumbled
¼ cup grated Parmesan cheese	Vegetable dippers or assorted crackers
1 tablespoon lemon juice	

In bowl mash avocado; stir in sour cream, Parmesan cheese, lemon juice, and salt. Turn into serving bowl. Cover and chill up to 2 hours. Sprinkle with crumbled bacon; serve with vegetables or crackers. Makes 1¼ cups.

Stuffed Cherry Tomatoes: Prepare Avocado Dip as above. Cut a thin slice from bottoms of about 40 *cherry tomatoes* so they sit flat. Cut a thin slice from tops. With melon baller or small spoon, carefully scoop out centers; discard. Sprinkle insides lightly with *salt* and *pepper.* Invert on paper toweling and chill. Fill each tomato with some of the Avocado Dip, using a small spoon; garnish with bacon, if desired. Makes 40.

Versatile Avocado Dip *can also be used to stuff mushroom caps for a delightful cold tidbit. Simply remove the stems from small fresh mushrooms, then spoon in a small amount of dip.*

For variety, alternate stuffed cherry tomatoes and mushrooms on a platter lined with leaf lettuce.

SHERRIED CHEESE BALL pictured on page 80

8 ounces sharp cheddar cheese	¼ teaspoon dry mustard
2 tablespoons butter or margarine	¼ cup toasted sesame seed
	Snipped parsley
⅓ cup milk	Assorted crackers and party rye bread
3 tablespoons dry sherry	

Cut cheese into cubes; allow cheese and butter or margarine to come to room temperature. Put *half* of the cheese into blender container; cover and blend till chopped. Remove and set aside; repeat with remaining cheese. Return all cheese to blender; add butter, milk, sherry, and mustard. Cover and blend with several on/off motions till smooth. Chill several hours. Form into a ball.

Roll cheese ball in sesame seed; garnish with snipped parsley. Chill; serve with crackers and bread. Makes 1 ball.

CREAMY CLAM DIP

1 7½-ounce can minced clams	¼ teaspoon garlic salt
2 3-ounce packages cream cheese, softened	Dash bottled hot pepper sauce
½ teaspoon Worcestershire sauce	½ cup shredded cheddar cheese
	Corn chips or crackers

Drain clams, reserving liquid. Beat cream cheese with 2 tablespoons reserved clam liquid, Worcestershire, garlic salt, and pepper sauce. Stir in clams, cheddar cheese, and enough clam liquid to make dipping consistency. Chill. Remove from refrigerator 15 minutes before serving. Serve with corn chips or crackers. Makes 1⅓ cups.

For more colorful Creamy Clam Dip, *substitute cream cheese with chives or cream cheese with pimientos for the plain cream cheese in the recipe.*

Serve an assortment of fresh fruit with Fruit Cheese Dip. *Apple wedges, bias-sliced bananas, pineapple chunks, pear slices, melon balls, whole strawberries, or cherries make appetizing dippers. Offer your guests a choice of flavor with this dip. Instead of the strawberry preserves, try apricot, red raspberry, or pineapple preserves.*

FRUIT-CHEESE DIP

1   3-ounce package cream
   cheese, softened
½   cup dairy sour cream
¼   cup strawberry preserves

1   teaspoon finely shredded
   lemon peel
1   tablespoon lemon juice
   Fruit dippers

In mixing bowl beat cream cheese till fluffy. Beat in sour cream, preserves, lemon peel, and juice till well mixed. Spear cut-up fruit on cocktail picks; dunk into dip. Makes about 1 cup.

CRAB-CHEESE FONDUE

1   8-ounce package cream
   cheese
½   cup dry white wine
1½ cups shredded Swiss cheese
   (6 ounces)
1   teaspoon cornstarch

1   7-ounce can crab meat
3   tablespoons milk
2   teaspoons Worcestershire
   sauce
1   teaspoon snipped parsley
   French bread, cubed

In saucepan over low heat melt together cream cheese and wine, stirring constantly. Toss Swiss cheese with cornstarch to coat. Drain crab; flake, removing cartilage. Stir crab, Swiss cheese, milk, Worcestershire sauce, and parsley into wine mixture in saucepan; heat through. Transfer to fondue pot or chafing dish; keep warm. Spear bread cubes with fondue fork; dip into fondue, swirling to coat. Makes about 3 cups.

Microwave cooking directions: In 4-cup glass measure cook cream cheese and wine in countertop microwave oven on high power for 2 minutes; stir every 30 seconds. Toss Swiss cheese with cornstarch. Drain crab; flake, removing cartilage. Stir crab, Swiss cheese, milk, Worcestershire, and parsley into wine mixture; micro-cook 3 minutes, stirring once. Transfer to fondue pot; serve as above.

The "hotness" of the taco sauce you choose for making Chili Con Queso *will determine the character of the dip. If you like your chili fiery, buy sauce labeled hot. If you prefer more subtle chili flavor, choose a mild sauce.*

CHILI CON QUESO   pictured on pages 68–69

1   8-ounce bottle taco sauce
1   4-ounce can green chili
   peppers, rinsed, seeded,
   and chopped
1   clove garlic, minced

2   cups shredded cheddar *or*
   Monterey Jack cheese
   (8 ounces)
   Celery sticks *or* tortilla chips

In saucepan heat taco sauce, chili peppers, and garlic to boiling; reduce heat and simmer for 5 minutes. Stir in cheese till melted. Transfer to fondue pot; keep warm. Use celery sticks or tortilla chips as dippers. Makes 1¾ cups.

Microwave cooking directions: In 4-cup glass measure combine taco sauce, chili peppers, and garlic. Cook in a countertop microwave oven on high power 3 minutes, stirring once. Stir in cheese; micro-cook 30 seconds more. Stir cheese till melted. Transfer to fondue pot. Serve as above.

BRAUNSCHWEIGER PÂTÉ

1 pound braunschweiger *or* liverwurst, broken up
1 8-ounce package cream cheese, softened
2 tablespoons milk
1 tablespoon grated onion

1 teaspoon chili powder
¼ teaspoon garlic salt
1 tablespoon milk
Few dashes bottled hot pepper sauce
Assorted crackers

Beat braunschweiger, *half* of cream cheese, 2 tablespoons milk, onion, chili powder, and garlic salt till smooth. Form into a ball; place on plate. Whip remaining cream cheese with 1 tablespoon milk and pepper sauce. Spread over braunschweiger; chill till firm. Sprinkle with snipped parsley, if desired. Serve with crackers. Makes 2¼ cups.

CHICKEN LIVER PÂTÉ

3 slices bacon
1 pound chicken livers
2 medium carrots, shredded
¼ cup chopped onion
2 tablespoons butter

2 tablespoons brandy
1 teaspoon salt
⅛ teaspoon pepper
⅛ teaspoon ground nutmeg
Assorted crackers

In skillet cook bacon till crisp; drain, reserving 2 tablespoons drippings in skillet. Crumble bacon; set aside. Add livers, carrots, and onion to skillet. Cook and stir 5 minutes or till livers are no longer pink and vegetables are tender. Remove from heat; stir in butter, brandy, salt, pepper, nutmeg, and bacon. Cool slightly. Turn about *half* at a time into blender container; cover and blend till smooth. Press into lightly oiled 2-cup mold; cover and chill. Turn out onto serving plate. Garnish with parsley, if desired. Serve with crackers. Makes 2 cups.

MUSHROOM SPREAD

4 slices bacon
8 ounces fresh mushrooms, chopped (3 cups)
1 onion, finely chopped
1 clove garlic, minced
2 tablespoons all-purpose flour
¼ teaspoon salt
⅛ teaspoon pepper

1 8-ounce package cream cheese, cubed
2 teaspoons Worcestershire sauce
1 teaspoon soy sauce
½ cup dairy sour cream
Party rye bread *or* crackers

In skillet cook bacon till crisp; drain, reserving 2 tablespoons drippings. Crumble bacon; set aside. Cook mushrooms, onion, and garlic in reserved drippings till tender and most of liquid evaporates. Stir in flour, salt, and pepper. Add cream cheese, Worcestershire, and soy. Cook and stir till cheese melts. Stir in sour cream and bacon. Heat through; do not boil. Serve warm with bread or crackers. Makes 2½ cups.

Break away from the traditional all-female bridal shower by inviting friends of both bride and groom to a wine shower. The guests bring a bottle of wine as their gift to the couple.

To make preparations easier for you, ask the guests to bring a favorite appetizer and the recipe for preparing it. At the party you provide the beverages, and the bride and groom will enjoy the party recipes in the future.

Suggest ideas for guests who don't have a favorite party snack. They'll appreciate the easy preparation of such recipes as Braunschweiger Pâté, Mushroom Spread, or Herbed Cheese Spread (see recipe, page 81).

Dill-Shrimp Dip, Sherried Cheese Ball (see recipe, page 77),
Herbed Cheese Spread, and Curried Chicken Spread

HERBED CHEESE SPREAD

1 8-ounce package cream cheese, softened	½ teaspoon dried thyme, crushed
¼ cup butter *or* margarine, softened	¼ teaspoon pepper
1 clove garlic, minced	Milk
	Assorted crackers

Beat together cream cheese, butter, garlic, thyme, and pepper. Let stand at room temperature 1 hour to blend flavors. Store in refrigerator. Let stand at room temperature 1 hour before serving to soften. Add milk, if necessary, to make of spreading consistency. Serve with crackers. Makes 1½ cups.

CURRIED CHICKEN SPREAD

1 cup chopped cooked chicken *or* two 5-ounce cans boned chicken, drained	1 8-ounce package cream cheese, softened
3 tablespoons chutney	2 tablespoons mayonnaise
2 green onions, cut up	1½ teaspoons curry powder
	Sliced pumpernickel bread

Grind together chicken, chutney, and onions. Beat together cream cheese, mayonnaise, and curry till fluffy. Fold in chicken mixture. Garnish with chopped peanuts, if desired. Spread on bread. Makes 2¼ cups.

DILL-SHRIMP DIP

1½ cups dairy sour cream	2 tablespoons milk
1 4½-ounce can shrimp, drained and chopped	1 tablespoon lemon juice
1 hard-cooked egg, chopped	1 teaspoon Worcestershire sauce
3 tablespoons thinly sliced green onion	½ teaspoon dried dillweed
	Vegetable dippers

Combine sour cream, shrimp, egg, onion, milk, lemon juice, Worcestershire, and dill; mix well. Cover and chill. Stir in a little additional milk, if needed. Serve with vegetable dippers. Makes about 2 cups.

GREEN GODDESS DIP

¾ cup dairy sour cream	1 tablespoon anchovy paste
½ cup mayonnaise	1 teaspoon lemon juice
¼ cup snipped parsley	1 clove garlic, minced
2 tablespoons snipped chives	Vegetable dippers

Mix sour cream, mayonnaise, parsley, chives, anchovy paste, lemon juice, and garlic. Cover; chill. Serve with vegetable dippers. Makes 1¼ cups.

Huge crackers make novel platters for appetizer spreads and crackers. Other foods also double as containers. Hollow a pattypan squash and pile in Curried Chicken Spread. *Pipe* Herbed Cheese Spread *into an unpeeled avocado half.*

Scooped-out tomatoes, green or red peppers, melon halves, and bread loaves may be used to hold similar spreads and dips. Using your imagination, you're bound to think of others.

Center your table of appetizers with a bowl of dip and vegetable dippers, and you won't need an additional centerpiece.

Raw vegetables of all colors and shapes can be arranged on a bed of lettuce, a tray of crushed ice, or a serving plate.

Include celery and carrot sticks, green pepper rings, radishes, cherry tomatoes, green onions, zucchini and cucumber spears, mushrooms, cauliflower flowerets, broccoli flowerets, turnip slices, green beans, and asparagus spears.

If jicama and kohlrabi are available in your area, add them to your tray.

The holiday season is the time to see friends in an informal setting. Schedule an open house for several hours in the afternoon, and serve foods such as these that need no attention during the party.

Cranberry Punch sets off the day with its brilliant red color. Add an ice ring made of lemonade and cranberries. Serves 12.

See index for recipe pages.

CRANBERRY PUNCH

1 cup boiling water	1 32-ounce bottle cranberry
1 3-ounce package	juice cocktail, chilled
raspberry-flavored gelatin	1 28-ounce bottle grapefruit
1 6-ounce can frozen lemonade	carbonated beverage,
concentrate	chilled
3 cups cold water	Ice or ice ring

Pour boiling water over the gelatin; stir to dissolve. Stir in lemonade concentrate. Pour into large punch bowl. Stir in cold water and cranberry juice cocktail. Slowly pour in grapefruit beverage; stir gently to mix. Add ice or an ice ring. Makes 24 (4-ounce) servings.

FRUIT PUNCH MIX

2 6-ounce cans frozen lemonade	1 6-ounce can frozen orange
concentrate	juice concentrate
1 6-ounce can frozen limeade	8 cups water
concentrate	¾ cup grenadine syrup

In 1-gallon pitcher or bowl combine frozen concentrates and water; stir in grenadine. Chill thoroughly. Serve as directed in the following recipes. Makes about 3 quarts punch mix.

Fruit Punch: (pictured on the cover and on page 85) Pour the punch mix into a large punch bowl; add *ice*. Slowly add two 32-ounce bottles *lemon-lime carbonated beverage or grapefruit carbonated beverage,* chilled. Makes 40 (4-ounce) servings.

Spiked Punch: Pour punch mix into punch bowl; add *ice* and one 750-milliliter bottle *light rum or vodka.* Slowly add one 28-ounce bottle *carbonated water,* chilled. Makes 40 (4-ounce) servings.

Wine Punch: Measure chilled punch mix into punch bowl. Add an equal quantity of chilled *white wine or champagne;* stir. Garnish with *strawberries,* if desired.

Individual Cocktails: Pour 1 jigger (1½ ounces) *rum, vodka, bourbon, or brandy* over *ice* in a tall glass. Add ½ cup punch mix; stir. Garnish with lemon, lime, or orange twist. Makes 24.

RASPBERRY PUNCH

1 pint raspberry sherbet	1 10-ounce package frozen
2 cups apple juice	raspberries
2 cups water	1 28-ounce bottle grapefruit
1 cup sugar	carbonated beverage or
1 cup lemon juice	ginger ale, chilled

Spoon sherbet into punch bowl. Combine apple juice, water, sugar, and lemon juice; stir till sugar dissolves. Add raspberries; stir till raspberries separate. Stir into sherbet in bowl. Slowly add carbonated beverage. Makes about 25 (4-ounce) servings.

SPARKLING ICED TEA PUNCH

8 tea bags	½ cup lemon juice
4 sprigs fresh mint leaves	1 28-ounce bottle carbonated
4 cups boiling water	water, chilled
½ cup sugar	Ice

Steep tea bags and mint leaves in boiling water for 5 minutes. Discard bags and mint. Add sugar to tea; stir till dissovled. Stir in lemon juice. Chill. Pour into punch bowl or 1-gallon pitcher. Slowly add carbonated water and ice. Makes 12 (5-ounce) servings.

VODKA PUNCH

1 46-ounce can pineapple-grapefruit juice, chilled	1 32-ounce bottle ginger ale, chilled
1½ cups vodka, chilled	Ice cubes *or* ice ring

In punch bowl combine juice and vodka. Slowly pour in ginger ale; stir gently. Add ice cubes or ice ring. Makes 25 (4-ounce) servings.

EGGNOG

2 eggs, separated	5½ cups milk
1 4-serving-size package *instant* vanilla pudding mix	¼ cup sugar
	1 teaspoon vanilla
	¼ teaspoon ground nutmeg

Beat egg whites till stiff peaks form. Combine egg yolks and remaining ingredients; beat smooth. Fold in egg whites. Chill; pour into glasses. Sprinkle with additional nutmeg, if desired. Makes 8 (6-ounce) servings.

Spiked Eggnog: Prepare Eggnog as above, *except* use 5 cups milk and add ½ cup *bourbon, rum, or brandy.*

CHOCOLATE-ORANGE SODAS

1 cup presweetened cocoa powder	1 quart vanilla ice cream
1 cup orange juice	3 cups orange carbonated beverage, chilled

Stir together cocoa powder and orange juice. Divide mixture into 6 tall glasses. To each glass add one or two scoops of ice cream; stir slightly. Carefully pour in carbonated beverage; stir. Serve with straws and long-handled spoons. Makes 6 servings.

Chocolate-Strawberry Sodas: Prepare Chocolate-Orange Sodas as above, *except* use *strawberry ice cream* and *strawberry carbonated beverage* instead of vanilla ice cream and orange carbonated beverage.

To make an attractive ice ring, alternate thin lime slices and maraschino cherries in a ring mold. Add just enough water or fruit juice to cover fruit; freeze. When frozen, fill mold with more water or juice and freeze again.

Use the same method to make ice rings with nearly any kind of fruit and fruit juice; try orange slices, lemon slices, pineapple chunks, cherries, strawberries, and peach slices.

To vary the color of the ring, add food coloring or choose a brightly colored canned fruit drink. Be sure the flavor is compatible with the punch.

When you have overnight guests, plan a late-morning brunch so no one has to wake up early. Here's a brunch menu that you can complete in less than 45 minutes.

Prepare the biscuits and roll them out. Place on baking sheet; put in oven about 15 minutes before serving time.

Meanwhile, prepare omelet. Reduce oven temperature when biscuits are done, and put omelet in for finishing. You'll have just enough time left to make the coolers and serve everything. Serves 6.

*See index for recipe pages

BUTTERMILK-FRUIT COOLERS

3 cups buttermilk	1 cup frozen unsweetened
2 to 3 tablespoons honey	sliced peaches,
1 teaspoon vanilla	strawberries, or
	blueberries

In blender container combine buttermilk, honey, and vanilla. Add frozen fruit; cover and blend 30 seconds or till smooth. Pour into glasses; garnish with fresh mint, if desired. Makes 6 (5-ounce) servings.

SUMMER ICE CREAM PUNCH

1 46-ounce can	1 28-ounce bottle ginger ale,
pineapple-orange juice,	chilled
chilled	1 pint orange or lemon sherbet
	or vanilla ice cream

For each serving, pour ½ cup pineapple-orange juice into a 10-ounce glass; add about ¼ cup ginger ale. Top with a scoop of sherbet or ice cream. Makes 12 (10-ounce) servings.

CHOCOLATE-MINT SHAKES

1 pint chocolate ice cream	¼ cup crème de menthe or
1 cup milk	mint jelly

In blender container combine ice cream, milk, and crème de menthe or jelly. Cover; blend just till mixed. Makes 4 (5-ounce) servings.

STRAWBERRY COOLER pictured on the cover

2 cups orange juice	1 cup pineapple juice
1 10-ounce package frozen	1½ cups carbonated water
strawberries, thawed	Ice cubes

In blender container place orange juice, strawberries, and pineapple juice; cover and blend till frothy. Stir in carbonated water; pour over ice in tall glasses. Makes 5 (8-ounce) servings.

Strawberry Slush: Prepare Strawberry Cooler as above, *except* do not add the carbonated water. Pour mixture into 9x9x2-inch pan; freeze solid. Remove from freezer and let stand at room temperature for 10 to 15 minutes. To make a slush, scrape spoon across surface of frozen mixture; spoon into bowl. Slowly add carbonated water; stir gently to mix. Spoon into glasses.

Fruit Punch (see recipe, page 82), Piña Colada (see recipe, page 91), Café Brûlot (see recipe, page 90), Summer Ice Cream Punch, Spiced Chocolate Sipper (see recipe, page 87), Strawberry Slush, and Gin and Tonic (see recipe, page 89)

Chilly Spiced Wine *also makes a warming hot spiced wine. Add the wine to the remaining ingredients after they have simmered for 10 minutes, then heat through.*

As guests arrive, greet them with steaming spiced wine with cinnamon stick stirrers or garnish with clove-studded orange slices.

CHILLY SPICED WINE

2 **cups cranberry-apple drink**
2 **tablespoons sugar**
8 **inches stick cinnamon, broken**

3 **whole cloves**
4 **cardamom pods, opened**
2 **cups dry red wine**
    Orange slices (optional)

In saucepan heat cranberry-apple drink, sugar, and spices to boiling; simmer 10 minutes. Strain spices. Stir in wine; cover and chill. Garnish with orange slices. Makes 5 (6 ounce) servings.

FRUITED CHAMPAGNE PUNCH

1 **46-ounce can unsweetened pineapple juice**
2 **6-ounce cans frozen pineapple-orange juice concentrate**

2 **12-ounce cans frozen lemonade concentrate**
8 **cups water**
3 **750-milliliter bottles champagne, chilled**

Stir pineapple juice into concentrates. Stir in water. Chill. Pour into punch bowl; slowly add champagne. Stir gently. Garnish with thin orange, lemon, or lime slices, if desired. Makes 50 (4-ounce) servings.

SANGRIA   pictured on pages 68–69

1 **750-milliliter bottle dry red *or* rosé wine**
2 **cups carbonated water**

2 **oranges**
2 **lemons *or* limes**
¼ **cup sugar**

Chill wine and carbonated water. Cut one orange and one lemon into slices. Squeeze juice from remaining fruits into a pitcher; stir in sugar. Stir in wine; add carbonated water and fruit slices. Serve in wine glasses. Makes 8 (6-ounce) servings.

During hot weather, chill Russian Tea *for a refreshing summer drink. Serve over ice in tall glasses with lemon wedges.*

RUSSIAN TEA

8 **tea bags**
6 **cups boiling water**
2 **cups orange juice**
½ **cup honey**

⅓ **cup lemon juice**
6 **whole cloves**
4 **inches stick cinnamon, broken**

Steep tea bags in boiling water for 5 minutes. Discard tea bags. Meanwhile, in large saucepan combine orange juice, honey, lemon juice, cloves, and stick cinnamon; bring to boiling. Reduce heat and simmer for 10 minutes. Add tea and heat through. Strain spices. Serve in mugs with lemon slices or additional cinnamon sticks, if desired. Makes 12 (6-ounce) servings.

FRUITED HONEY-YOGURT NOG

1 8-ounce carton plain *or* flavored yogurt	⅓ cup honey
1 cup water	1 egg
1 6-ounce can frozen fruit juice concentrate	1½ teaspoons vanilla
	8 to 12 ice cubes
	Orange slices (optional)

In blender container place yogurt, water, frozen concentrate, honey, egg, and vanilla. Cover and blend about 1 minute or till smooth. Through opening in lid of blender (or with lid slightly ajar) add ice cubes one at a time while blending; blend till smooth. Pour into tall glasses; garnish with orange slices. Makes 5 (6-ounce) servings.

Fruited Honey-Yogurt Nog can become any flavor you like by changing the frozen fruit juice concentrate you use. Try orange, apple, pineapple, grape, grapefruit, tangerine, or cranberry.

Serve this nutritious drink as a quick breakfast in a glass, as a snack, or as a dessert.

SPICED CHOCOLATE SIPPER   pictured on page 85

6 cups milk	¼ teaspoon ground cardamom
⅔ cup chocolate-flavored syrup	1 tablespoon vanilla
3 tablespoons honey	½ cup brandy (optional)
½ teaspoon ground nutmeg	Whipped cream

In a large saucepan heat milk with chocolate-flavored syrup, honey, ground nutmeg, and ground cardamom till small bubbles form around the edge of the pan. Remove milk-chocolate mixture from heat; stir in vanilla. Add brandy, if desired. Serve in mugs; top with dollops of whipped cream. Garnish with chocolate curls, if desired. Makes 7 (8-ounce) servings.

GLÖGG

Peel from one orange (white portion removed)	2 750-milliliter bottles sweet red wine
8 inches stick cinnamon, broken	2 cups gin, vodka, *or* aquavit
12 whole cloves	1 cup raisins
4 cardamom pods, opened	¼ cup honey
	1 cup blanched whole almonds

For spice bag, tie orange peel, cinnamon, cloves, and cardamom in cheesecloth. In large saucepan or kettle combine wine, gin, vodka, or aquavit, raisins, honey and spice bag. Heat to simmering; simmer 5 to 10 minutes. *Do not boil.* If desired, hold at room temperature for 2 to 3 hours to develop more flavor; reheat. Remove spice bag. Add almonds just before serving. Makes 16 (4-ounce) servings.

Crockery cooker directions: Combine all ingredients except almonds in electric slow crockery cooker. Cover and heat on low-heat setting for 4 to 6 hours. Remove spice bag. Add almonds just before serving.

Your crockery cooker is just the thing for serving hot beverages to large groups. Keep it on the low-heat setting for as long as you like.

BASIC BAR GUIDE

If you think bartending requires a degree in mixology, relax, because it doesn't. All you need is an adequate supply of liquor and mixers.
Experience is the best clue to the type and quantity of supplies you'll need, so watch your friends at an earlier occasion to note their preferences.
If you have no idea what your guests will drink, obtain the basics: whiskey, Scotch, gin, vodka, rum, and vermouth for cocktails; wine and beer to drink alone. Add sherry, tequila, liqueurs, and alternate liquor brands when budget and storage space allow.
On the average, expect guests to drink 1 to 3 cocktails each hour. A liter bottle of liquor makes twenty 1½-ounce servings of liquor.

To complete your bar supplies, buy plenty of mixers: carbonated water, tonic water, ginger ale, cola, and other beverages (for non-drinkers, too); lemons and limes for juice and twists; fruit juices; and sugar. And don't forget you'll need water and plenty of ice.
To chill a drink without watering it, prechill liquors and mixers. Chill glasses in freezer or fill with ice and empty before adding the drink.
Finish each drink with a creative garnish: green olives, cocktail onions, maraschino cherries, or fresh fruit wedges or slices.
Don't let the ounce measures confuse you. A jigger is handy for measuring 1½ ounces, a pony for 1 ounce. Use a tablespoon measure for ½ ounce, 1½ teaspoons for ¼ ounce.

martini

Combine 2 ounces dry *gin*, ½ ounce *dry vermouth*, and *cracked ice*. Stir; strain into chilled cocktail glass. Garnish with a *lemon twist or* an *olive*. Makes 1.

DRY MARTINI: Prepare Martini as above, *except* use only ¼ ounce dry vermouth.

SWEET MARTINI: Prepare Martini as above, *except* add ½ ounce *sweet vermouth* with dry vermouth.

gibson

Prepare your favorite martini; garnish with a *pearl onion* instead of lemon twist or olive.

manhattan

Mix 1½ ounces blended *whiskey*, ½ ounce *sweet vermouth*, dash *bitters*, and *cracked ice*. Strain. Garnish with *maraschino cherry*. Makes 1.

DRY MANHATTAN: Prepare Manhattan as above, *except* substitute *dry vermouth* for sweet vermouth. Garnish with *olive*.

PERFECT MANHATTAN: Prepare Manhattan as above, *except* add ½ ounce *dry vermouth* with the sweet vermouth.

bourbon sour

In cocktail shaker combine 2 ounces *bourbon, Scotch, or rye whiskey;* 1 ounce *lemon or lime juice;* and 2 teaspoons *powdered sugar*. Add *ice cubes* and shake well. Strain into chilled glass. Add 1 ounce *grapefruit carbonated beverage;* add *ice cubes*, if desired. Garnish with *lemon slice* and *maraschino cherry*. Makes 1.

VODKA SOUR: Prepare Bourbon Sour as above, *except* substitute 2 ounces *vodka* for the bourbon.

amaretto sour

In cocktail shaker combine 2 ounces *Amaretto* and 1 ounce *lemon or lime juice*. Add *ice cubes* and shake well. Strain into a chilled glass. Add 1 ounce *grapefruit carbonated beverage;* add *ice cubes*, if desired. Garnish with *lemon slice* and *maraschino cherry*. Makes 1.

collins

In a tall glass stir together 1½ teaspoons *sugar or Simple Syrup* and 1 ounce *lemon juice*. Add 1½ ounces *gin, vodka, or rum;* stir to mix well. Fill glass with *ice cubes*. Add 6 ounces chilled *carbonated water* to fill glass. Garnish with *orange slice* and *maraschino cherry*. Makes 1.

gin and tonic

Pitcher of Gin and Tonics pictured on pages 68–69. Pour 2 ounces *gin* into a glass. Add *ice cubes;* pour in about 4 ounces *tonic water* (quinine water) to fill glass. Squeeze a *lime wedge* into glass, then add wedge to drink. Makes 1.

VODKA AND TONIC: Prepare Gin and Tonic as above, *except* substitute 2 ounces *vodka* for gin.

bloody mary

In cocktail shaker combine 3 ounces *tomato juice*, 1½ ounces *vodka*, ½ ounce *lemon juice*, dash *Worcestershire sauce*, dash *celery salt*, dash *pepper or* bottled *hot pepper sauce*, and *ice cubes*. Shake. Pour into a glass with or without additional ice cubes. Garnish with a *lemon wedge or celery stalk*. Makes 1.

NOTE: You may prefer to make Bloody Mary ahead and chill for flavors to blend. Stir before serving.

screwdriver

Place 3 or 4 *ice cubes* in a tall 8-ounce glass. Add 2 ounces *vodka* and ½ ounce *orange liqueur* (optional). Add 4 to 6 ounces *orange juice* to fill the glass; stir. Garnish with *orange wedge or maraschino cherry*. Makes 1.

harvey wallbanger

In tall glass combine 1 ounce *vodka* and ½ ounce *Galliano*. Stir in 6 ounces *orange juice* and fill glass with ice cubes. Garnish with *orange slice*. Makes 1.

margarita

In cocktail shaker combine 1½ ounces *tequila*, 1 ounce *lime juice*, and 1 ounce *orange liqueur*. Add *ice cubes* and shake well. For salt-rimmed glass, rub the rim of a cocktail glass with a *lime wedge* to moisten. Invert glass into a dish of *coarse salt* to make a salted rim. Strain into the glass. Makes 1.

FROZEN MARGARITA: Pictured on pages 68–69. In blender container combine 6 ounces *tequila*, 4 ounces *lime juice*, and 4 ounces *orange liqueur*. Cover and blend till smooth. With blender running, add 20 to 24 *ice cubes*, one at a time, through hole in lid, blending till drink is a slushy mixture. Serve immediately in salt-rimmed glasses. Makes 4.

tequila sunrise

Pour 1½ ounces *tequila* and ½ ounce *lime juice* over *crushed ice* in a tall glass. Slowly pour in 3 ounces *orange juice*. Pour in ¼ ounce *grenadine syrup*. Garnish with a *lime slice*. Stir before drinking. Makes 1.

kir

Pour 6 ounces chilled dry *white wine* into a chilled wine glass. Add ½ ounce *crème de cassis;* stir gently to mix. Add *ice cubes,* if desired. Garnish with *lemon twist.* Makes 1.

wine spritzer

In tall glass place a *lemon twist.* Fill glass with *ice cubes* or *Fruited Ice Cubes.* Pour in 4 ounces chilled dry *white wine* and 2 ounces chilled *carbonated water;* stir gently to mix. Garnish with fresh *strawberries or* a *lemon or lime slice.* Makes 1.

FRUITED ICE CUBES: Place 1 *strawberry or lemon twist* in each compartment of ice cube tray. Add *water* and freeze into cubes.

orange champagne

Thinly peel ½ of an *orange* into a spiral about 12 inches long; place peel in chilled champagne glass. Add 2 teaspoons *orange liqueur;* pour in 4 ounces chilled *champagne.* Stir gently to mix. Makes 1.

daiquiri

In cocktail shaker combine 1½ ounces light *rum,* 1 ounce *lime juice,* 1 teaspoon *powdered sugar,* 1 teaspoon *orange liqueur* (optional), and *cracked ice.* Shake well; strain into chilled cocktail glass. Makes 1.

FROZEN DAIQUIRI: In blender container combine 3 ounces light *rum,* 2 ounces *lime juice,* 1 tablespoon *powdered sugar,* and 2 teaspoons *orange liqueur.* With blender running, add 11 or 12 *ice cubes,* one at a time, through hole in lid, blending till drink is a slushy mixture. Pour into 2 chilled wine glasses without straining. Makes 2.

fruit daiquiris

STRAWBERRY DAIQUIRIS: In blender container combine one 10-ounce package frozen sliced *strawberries,* broken up, with ¾ cup light *rum* and ½ cup frozen *lemonade concentrate.* Cover and blend till smooth. With blender running, add 20 to 24 *ice cubes,* one at a time through hole in lid, to make about 5 cups slushy mixture. (If mixture becomes too thick, add a little water.) Pour into glasses. Makes 4 (10-ounce) servings.

PEACH DAIQUIRIS: In blender container combine one 12-ounce package frozen unsweetened *peach slices,* ¾ cup light *rum,* ½ cup frozen *lemonade concentrate,* and ⅓ cup sifted *powdered sugar.* Cover and blend till smooth. With blender running, add 20 to 24 *ice cubes,* one at a time through hole in lid, to make about 5 cups slushy mixture. (If mixture becomes too thick, add a little water.) Makes 4 (10-ounce) servings.

PINEAPPLE DAIQUIRIS: In blender container combine one 8-ounce can *crushed pineapple* in syrup, ¾ cup light *rum,* and ½ cup frozen *pineapple-orange juice concentrate.* Cover and blend till smooth. With blender running, add 20 to 24 *ice cubes,* one at a time through hole in lid, to make 5 cups slushy mixture. (If mixture becomes too thick, add a little water.) Makes 4 (10-ounce) servings.

APPLE DAIQUIRIS: In blender container combine one 6-ounce can frozen *apple juice concentrate,* ¾ cup light *rum,* 2 tablespoons *lime juice,* and ¼ teaspoon ground *cinnamon.* Add 2 *apples,* peeled, cored, and cut up. Cover and blend till smooth. With blender running, add 20 to 24 *ice cubes,* one at a time through hole in lid, to make 5 cups slushy mixture. (If mixture becomes too thick, add a little water.) Makes 4 (10-ounce) servings.

hot buttered rum

Beat together ¾ cup packed *brown sugar,* ½ cup softened *butter or margarine,* ¼ teaspoon ground *cinnamon,* ¼ teaspoon ground *allspice,* and ¼ teaspoon finely shredded *lemon peel.* Use immediately or cover and chill till needed.

To serve, place a rounded tablespoon of the brown sugar mixture in each 8-ounce mug. Add 1½ ounces dark *rum to each* mug; fill *each* with *boiling water.* Garnish with whole *cloves* and *lemon slices,* if desired. Makes 10 (6-ounce) servings.

mocha toddies

Combine one 2-ounce jar (¾ cup) *instant coffee crystals* and ¼ cup *hot water;* stir to dissolve coffee. Add one 16-ounce can (1½ cups) *chocolate-flavored syrup,* 1 cup *rum,* and 1 tablespoon *vanilla.* Use immediately or cover and chill till needed.

For *each serving,* stir 2 tablespoons coffee mixture into ¾ cup hot *milk* in mug. Top with a scoop of *vanilla ice cream.* Makes 22 (6-ounce) servings.

café brulot

Brew coffee double strength, using 3 cups *water,* ⅓ to ½ cup *ground coffee,* and 4 inches *stick cinnamon,* broken. Remove coffee grounds and cinnamon; keep coffee hot.

In flameproof bowl combine the *peel from 1 orange* (white portion removed), 6 whole *cloves,* and 1 tablespoon *sugar.* Warm ½ cup *brandy or cognac* in a small pan; pour into bowl. Ignite with a long match. Stir brandy with a long-handled spoon for 2 minutes. Add the hot coffee; carefully stir till flame disappears. Strain into demitasse cups. Makes 6 (4-ounce) servings.

mint julep

Pour ½ ounce *Simple Syrup* into tall glass. Add 2 to 4 sprigs fresh *mint* and crush with back of spoon. Fill glass with *crushed ice*. Add 3 ounces *bourbon* and stir gently. Add more ice to fill glass. Sprinkle with *powdered sugar*. Garnish with *lemon slice* and *mint sprig*. Makes 1.

SIMPLE SYRUP: Pour 1 cup *boiling water* over 1 cup granulated *sugar*; stir till sugar dissolves. Chill.

julep punch

Combine one 10-ounce jar *mint jelly* and 2 cups *water*. Stir over low heat till jelly melts; cool. Add one 46-ounce can unsweetened *pineapple juice*, one 750-milliliter bottle *bourbon*, 2 cups *water*, and ½ cup *lime juice*; chill. Pour over *ice* in punch bowl. Pour in two 28-ounce bottles *lemon-lime carbonated beverage*, chilled. Garnish with fresh *mint* and *lime*. Makes 30 (6-ounce) servings.

planter's punch

In cocktail shaker combine 2 ounces *dark rum*, 1½ ounces unsweetened *pineapple juice*, 1½ ounces *orange juice*, ½ ounce *lemon or lime juice*, ½ ounce *Simple Syrup* (see recipe, above), dash *grenadine syrup*, and *ice cubes*. Shake; strain into ice-filled tall glass. Garnish with *Fruit Kebab*. Makes 1.

FRUIT KEBAB: Thread on a short skewer pieces of *pineapple*, *banana*, *orange*, *lime*, *lemon*, or *maraschino cherry*.

rusty nail

In glass combine 2 ounces *Scotch whiskey* and 1 ounce *Drambuie*. Add 2 *ice cubes;* stir. Makes 1.

gimlet

In cocktail shaker combine 1½ ounces *gin or vodka* with ½ ounce *sweetened lime juice* and *ice cubes*. Shake well; strain into chilled cocktail glass. Makes 1.

tomato beers

In tall glass pour ½ of a 12-ounce can (¾ cup) chilled *beer*. Add ⅓ cup chilled *hot-style tomato juice;* stir gently to mix. Add green onion stirrer. Makes 1.

mai tai

In a tall glass mix 1½ ounces *orange juice*, 1½ ounces unsweetened *pineapple juice*, 1 ounce *light rum*, 1 ounce *dark rum*, 1 ounce *sweetened lime juice*, and ½ ounce *orange liqueur*. Add enough *cracked ice* to fill glass; stir. If desired, garnish the glass with a thin slice of *lime* and fresh *mint*. Makes 1.

piña colada

Place 2 ounces chilled unsweetened *pineapple juice or* ¼ cup chilled canned *crushed pineapple with juice* in a blender container. Add 1½ ounces *rum*, 2 tablespoons *coconut cream*, and ¼ cup *cracked ice*. Cover and blend till well mixed. Pour into chilled cocktail glass. Garnish with a *pineapple spear*. Makes 1.

velvet hammer

In blender container combine 1½ ounces *white crème de cacao*, 1½ ounces *orange liqueur*, and 1 cup *vanilla ice cream*. Cover and blend till well mixed. Makes 2 (5-ounce) servings.

grasshopper

In cocktail shaker combine 1 ounce *white crème de cacao*, 1 ounce *green crème de menthe*, and 1 ounce *whipping cream*. Add *ice cubes;* shake vigorously till frothy. Strain into chilled cocktail glass. Makes 1.

ICE CREAM GRASSHOPPER: In blender container combine 1 ounce white *crème de cacao*, 1 ounce *green crème de menthe*, and ½ cup *vanilla ice cream*. Cover and blend just till smooth. Pour into glass. Makes 1.

CHOCOLATE GRASSHOPPER: In blender container combine 1 ounce *brown crème de cacao*, 1 ounce *white crème de menthe*, and ½ cup *chocolate ice cream*. Cover and blend just till smooth. Makes 1.

brandy alexander

In cocktail shaker combine 2 ounces *brandy*, 1 ounce *crème de cacao*, and 1 ounce *whipping cream*. Add 3 *ice cubes;* shake vigorously till frothy. Strain into chilled cocktail glass. Sprinkle with ground *nutmeg*. Makes 1.

ICE CREAM ALEXANDER: In blender container combine 1 ounce *brandy*, ½ ounce *crème de cacao*, and ½ cup *vanilla ice cream*. Cover and blend. Pour into glass; sprinkle with ground *nutmeg*. Makes 1.

black russian

Stir together 2 ounces *vodka* and 1 ounce *coffee liqueur*. If desired, serve over ice. Makes 1.

white russian

Stir together 2 ounces *vodka* and 1 ounce *coffee liqueur;* stir in 1½ ounces *light cream*. Pour over *ice* in glass. Makes 1.

WINE GUIDE

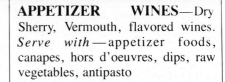

Wine is gaining favor at all types of gatherings, from barbecues to cocktail parties to sit-down dinners. This popularity brings with it a relaxing of traditional rules that once governed wine service. Today, the one important rule is to enjoy wine.

Wines fall into four general classifications according to when they are served. **APPETIZER WINES** are served before a meal or as a cocktail. **DINNER WINES** include red, white, and rosé wines, usually served with the main course. In general, red wines are dry and rich, white wines are lighter in flavor and can be dry or sweet, and rosé wines are pale red wines that may be dry or sweet.

DESSERT WINES are heavier in body and sweeter than dinner wines, and serve as a dessert or a dessert accompaniment.

SPARKLING WINES, served alone or with food, make any occasion special—before, during, or after a meal.

The information at the right indicates some foods and wines that harmonize. However, you are free to experiment with your own favorite foods and wines.

When buying wine for a party, choose larger bottles to economize. Plan on one 1½-liter bottle to serve 4 guests (6 to 8 guests, if it will be served only during a meal). Sample a smaller bottle to ensure a good choice before investing in large ones.

Store unopened wines at a cool constant temperature (about 60°) away from heat and light. Place a corked bottle on its side to keep the cork moist.

Pour dinner wines into 8- to 10-ounce wine glasses ½ to ⅔ full; serve smaller portions of appetizer and dessert wines.

APPETIZER WINES—Dry Sherry, Vermouth, flavored wines.
Serve with—appetizer foods, canapes, hors d'oeuvres, dips, raw vegetables, antipasto

RED DINNER WINES—Burgundy, Pinot Noir, Cabernet Sauvignon, Zinfandel, Gamay, Chianti, Petite Sirah, Barbera, Baco Noir
Serve with—Hearty foods, beef, pork, game, duck, goose, cheese and pasta dishes, highly seasoned meats and casseroles

ROSÉ DINNER WINES—Grenache Rosé, Rosé of Cabernet Sauvignon, Zinfandel Rosé, Rosé of Pinot Noir
Serve with—Ham, fried chicken, shellfish, cold beef, picnic foods, buffet foods

WHITE DINNER WINES—Chablis, Dry Sauterne, Rhine, Chardonnay, Chenin Blanc, White Riesling, French Colombard, Sauvignon Blanc, Seyval Blanc
Serve with—Light foods, chicken, turkey, fish, shellfish, ham, veal, chicken and fish salads

DESSERT WINES—Port, Sweet Sauterne, Muscat, Catawba, Aurora, Cream Sherry
Serve with—desserts, fruits, nuts, dessert cheeses, cakes, pies, tarts, cookies

SPARKLING WINES—Champagne, Cold Duck, Sparkling Burgundy, Sparkling Rosé
Serve with—all foods at any type of occasion

INDEX

C

D–F